WARPLANES
CHRISTOPHER CHANT

WARPLANES
CHRISTOPHER CHANT

MICHAEL JOSEPH
LONDON

ISBN 0 7181 2180 5

First published in Great Britain by
Michael Joseph Ltd.,
44 Bedford Square,
London WC1 B 3DU.
1983

Produced by Winchmore Publishing Services
Ltd.,
48 Lancaster Avenue,
Hadley Wood,
Herts,
England.

Edited by Sue Butterworth
Designed by Lawrence Bradbury
Picture Research Johnathan Moore

Printed in Hong Kong

CONTENTS

INTRODUCTION
6

THE FIGHTER
1918-1939
10

THE FIGHTER
1939-1961
30

THE BOMBER AND
ATTACK AIRCRAFT
118

INDEX
190

INTRODUCTION

WAR IS THE GREATEST SPUR to technological progress, and this simple truism is especially true of the First World War. For although there had been major wars in the previous 50 years (the Franco-Prussian War of 1870–1871, the 2nd Boer War of 1899–1902 and the Russo-Japanese War of 1904–1905 to name but three examples), their shortness or geographical remoteness had prevented the full impact of ever-hastening technological advance from impinging on them. Yet these 50 years had seen a technological transformation of the world, and it was only natural (though generally unforeseen by the protagonists) that any major conflict between technologically advanced countries would reflect this change.

Warfare was radically altered by technology between 1914 and 1918: some of the weapons had already made their appearance before the 'Great War', but their development in this conflict, and combination with other weapons, brought a different complexion to armed conflict. Such weapons are now commonplace, or at least accepted, but were terrifying novelties for the protagonists of the First World War: the submarine, the machine-gun, barbed wire, the flame thrower, poison gases of various kinds, the tank, wireless telegraphy, a host of other devices – and the aeroplane. This last

had made its debut as a weapon of war in the colonial struggle between Italy and Turkey for Tripoli in 1911 and 1912, presaging many of the roles undertaken by aircraft of a later generation, but having no real effect on the course of Italy's conquest of her first North African territory.

The aircraft of 1914 were flimsy machines of very limited capabilities. The only practical use envisaged for them was reconnaissance, but even with a payload of just two men their performance was limited to a gentle climb to an altitude of a few thousand feet, where a cruising speed of 50 mph (80 km/h) was considered good – and woe betide any luckless aviator who found himself faced with a headwind when he turned for home, as this was likely to reduce his speed over the ground to virtually nothing, and so to cause him to run out of fuel on the wrong side of the lines. Even so, worthwhile results were achieved by these primitive reconnaissance machines, leading to the inevitable conclusion that if it was worth one side expending money, effort and men to obtain something, then surely it was worth the comparable expense for the other side to prevent this. And so was born the fighter aircraft, designed to tackle other aircraft in aerial combat. At the same time, the first war-spurred advances in design,

engine power and reliability, and tactical thinking led to the evolution of aircraft capable of carrying a load significantly larger than just the crew and light weapons: so there appeared the bomber (to drop free-fall bombs or a torpedo), the artillery observation aircraft (able to communicate effectively with the gun crews whose work it was supervising), the attack aircraft (carrying small bombs and several well-supplied machine-guns for assaults on enemy infantry), the maritime patrol aircraft (with a considerable fuel load to provide long endurance) and a number of other types. Roles proliferated greatly by 1918, and the capabilities of aircraft increased markedly, though basic design factors remained little altered from those of 1914. Performance did improve by a considerable margin, and this can be attributed mainly to improved structural design coupled with increased power from the inline piston engines that had taken over as primary powerplants from the rotary piston engines. A simple comparison of average types of 1914 and 1918 reveals the technical advances made during the First World War: the British Royal Aircraft Factory B.E.2b was powered by a 70-hp (52.2-kW) Renault inline, had a maximum take-off weight of

1,600 lb (726 kg), carried no armament and could fly its two crew for 3 hours at a maximum speed of 72 mph (116 km/h); a comparable reconnaissance aircraft of 1918 was the Breguet 14 A.2, which was powered by a 320-hp (239-kW) Renault 12Fe inline, had a maximum take-off weight of 3,389 lb (1,537 kg), carried an armament of one fixed and two flexibly-mounted 0.303-in (7.7-mm) machine-guns and four 120-mm (4.72-in) bombs, and could fly its two crew in greater safety and comfort for an identical 3 hours with a maximum speed of 116 mph (187 km/h).

However, although enormous technological strides had been made in aviation during the First World War, and though a number of radical innovations (supercharged engines, metal construction, monoplane configuration, cannon armament etc) had appeared, these had gained no real currency. The aircraft of 1918 looked not too dissimilar from those of 1914: they were braced biplanes, generally of wooden construction with internal wire bracing and fabric covering, perched on fixed tailwheel type landing gear and offering the crew little protection from the elements or the enemy. But the aeroplane had been blooded in war – and its story was just beginning.

By comparison with aircraft dating from later in the First World War, the Royal Aircraft Factory B.E.2a of 1913 was a flimsy machine capable of only the most limited military flights for reconnaissance purposes. The aircraft illustrated was the first British military aircraft to land in France after the beginning of the First World War, and the pilot is seen recovering from the rigours of his cross-Channel flight in the bottom right-hand corner.

THE FIGHTER
1918-1939

Previous page: Last of the RAF's biplane fighters, the Gloster Gladiator offered a number of refinements in comparison with the Gloster Gauntlet it superseded, these including an enclosed cockpit, trailing-edge flaps, cantilever main landing gear legs, and an armament of two fuselage- and two wing-mounted machine-guns.

Below: The Armstrong Whitworth Siskin was clearly derived from the factors that dominated the design of fighters in the First World War. Seen here is an example of the Siskin IIIA(DC), a two-seat trainer version with dual controls.

THE FIRST WORLD WAR HAD A DUAL LEGACY so far as military aviation was concerned: the existence of large numbers of modern aircraft, and the near bankruptcy of virtually every country likely to need military aircraft within the foreseeable future. The inevitable result of this combination of factors was the abandonment of all but the most limited aeronautical development and procurement. The air forces of the victorious Allies, which had grown enormously between 1916 and 1918, were cut back drastically, and their remnants instructed to make do with the aircraft on hand. In this respect, therefore, the result of the war was that there remained in service for several years types which would otherwise have had operational lives of perhaps only one year: the British, for example, kept in service to 1926 the Sopwith 7F.1 Snipe, which had entered service in 1918; and the French kept in first-line service up to 1929 the Nieuport 29, which had been designed in 1918 but entered service just after the armistice.

All aircraft-manufacturing nations realised, however, that even if financial cutbacks and the presence of large numbers of war-surplus aircraft meant almost no funds for large scale procurement, some funding had to be devoted to keeping abreast of the aeronautical art, now being pushed on by the development of machines for the civil market. So countries such as France, Italy, the UK and the USA contented themselves with small-scale purchases of advanced types so that manufacturers (of both airframes and engines) would be kept in business, and their air forces gain experience with at least some of the latest technological developments. The first of these, and one that had been under development during the war, was the radial engine: compared with the inline, this was more compact in length, was potentially more reliable as it was less complex, and possessed a better power-to-weight ratio as it was free of the weight of the water and its associated plumbing that was so much of a feature of liquid-cooled inline engines. Wartime developments had not borne immediate fruit, but by the early 1920s the radial engine was sufficiently reliable for use in civil and military aircraft.

ARMSTRONG WHITWORTH SISKIN

The fighter that best epitomises this initial transition from the standards of the First World War was a stalwart of the Royal Air Force during the 1920s, the Armstrong Whitworth Siskin, powered initially by a 340-hp (254-kW) ABC Dragonfly radial. This engine had been developed during the closing stages of the war, and had great potential that was, unfortunately, never realised. The airframe origins of the Siskin also stretched back to the war years, but the development of the type and the 325-hp (242-kW) Armstrong Siddeley Jaguar radial that was finally selected to power it took the programme into the 1920s. But to a certain extent this protracted development played into the hands of the manufacturer, for it was in the early 1920s that the Air Ministry came to a far-reaching conclusion about airframes for future British service aircraft: henceforward the primary structure was to be of metal rather than of wood.

The reasoning for this change was based not on considerations of structural strength (contemporary wooden structures having a better strength-to-weight ratio than metal ones), but rather on supply and maintenance factors. During the First World War, the extensive aircraft-manufacturing programme of the UK had threatened to exhaust the supply of seasoned timber suitable for the task, and considerable problems had been encountered when improperly seasoned timber had been used. The Air Ministry thus reasoned that non-wooden structures would be safer for mass-production in the event of further large scale hostilities, and ordained that from 1924 RAF aircraft would have to be based on a metal airframe structure.

Thus the definitive Siskin III, which entered service in 1924, had been redesigned around a metal airframe and proved an admirable fighter. Some 70 Siskin IIIs were followed by about 350 Siskin IIIAs with the uprated Jaguar IVS, rated at 400 hp (298 kW). The Siskin IIIA served as a front-line British fighter up to 1932, when it was replaced by more advanced biplane types. The type was an advance over the First World War types, but only in detail rather than in concept: it adhered to the classic biplane fighter configuration, and was armed with the standard pair of rifle-calibre machine-guns. But it had considerably more power than its antecedents, and generally superior performance, though this latter was eroded by the relatively heavier metal structure. The fighters of 1918 had been designed for dog-fighting at low and medium altitudes, and were notably crisp (quite often dangerously so) in their control responsiveness; tactical thinking in the peacetime 1920s emphasised a greater versatility, so the Siskin could not match the all-out agility of machines such as the Sopwith 2F.1 Camel: however, it had excellent fields of vision for the pilot thanks to the adoption of a sesquiplane (large top wing with a lower wing smaller in span and chord), and markedly superior standards of equipment, especially for flight at night and at high altitude (exhaust flame dampers, cockpit heating, oxygen and radio).

The sesquiplane configuration of the Siskin IIIA is abundantly clear in this shot of the type. Less evident are features that marked it as an aircraft of post-First World War origins, notably the supercharger for the Armstrong Siddeley Jaguar IVS radial, which raised service ceiling to 27,000 ft (8,230 m).

Though its profusion of bracing wires clearly did much to reduce overall performance, the Siskin IIIA was a worthy successor to First World War fighters in its agility. The greatest display of the type's manoeuvrability possibly came in the 1930 Hendon RAF Display, when No. 43 Squadron performed a complex series of manoeuvres with the tips of its aircraft's wings tied together with cord. The limited production of the period is indicated by a total production of 412 by no fewer than five companies including the parent organisation.

BOEING F4B AND P12

One method of keeping down costs, and therefore of maximising a production run, is to produce a design so full of development potential that a large number of generations can be evolved from it: with each generation introducing perhaps one or two major component alterations, such a family can be kept fairly constantly at the forefront of technological development with minimal financial and aerodynamic risk. Not surprisingly, such a series commends itself to all treasury-controlled governments (particularly the present regime in Russia), and was admirably suited to the parsimony of an increasingly isolationist and pacifist USA

in the 1920s and early 1930s. Both Boeing and Curtiss succeeded in developing such families of fighters, though there can be little doubt that Boeing had the last word in revenue terms, producing some truly classic fighters. The starting point of the series was the Boeing Model 15, a sesquiplane prototype that led to the inline-engined PW-9 for the US Army and the FB-1 for the US Navy. Successive improvements kept the family in production, and with its Model 83 and Model 89 prototypes the company produced the component portions of the definitive Model 100, which led to the great P-12 for the US Army and the F4B for the US Navy. These two types, in various marks and with a small number for export, were eventually built to the tune of over 550 examples.

The PW-9/FB series had been fitted with tapered wings and inline engines, which the F2B changed by introducing a radial engine

Painted erroneously in the markings of a US Navy squadron, which did not use the type, this restored Boeing F4B-4 epitomises the trim radial-powered biplane fighters flown by the US Navy and US Marine Corps during the late 1920s and early 1930s.

The Boeing F2B-1 introduced to service with the US Navy the Pratt & Whitney Wasp radial engine. This type of engine was, for a given power output, lighter than a comparable inline engine (thanks to the absence of the radiator, coolant fluid and relevant plumbing) and also more reliable as it was less complex. The advantages for fighting aircraft were obvious, and they appealed most to the US Navy, which was of course restricted aboard its carriers with regard to the quantity of spares that could be accommodated.

(the 425-hp/317-kW Pratt & Whitney R-1340 Wasp radial, one of the most significant engines in the development of aviation) and the F3B by the introduction of new wings with constant chord, the upper wing being swept back quite sharply and the lower wing remaining straight. The PW-9/FB series ended service in 1925, the F2B/F3B derivative in 1928, and the ultimate P-12/F4B generation in 1929. A later version of the Wasp, offering slightly more power, made possible the necessary improvement in performance (maximum speed of the F4B-1 initial production version being 176 mph/ 283 km/h at 6,000 ft/1,830 m compared with the F3B-1's 156 mph/251 km/h at sea-level), while a general tidying up of the design made the later aircraft more compact than its predecessor, with consequent improvements in handling. In fact, the F4B-1 marked a slight return towards the standards of the First World War, with exceptionally rapid control response and absolute precision of manoeuvre, totally unmarred by the viciousness that had characterised some earlier designs. Improvements in later versions included a Townend ring round the previously exposed cylinder heads to reduce drag, and a semi-monocoque fuselage built up of dural (aluminium alloy) to replace the F4B-1's structure of bolted-up aluminium tube covered with fabric. The models that introduced these features were the P-12C and P-12E respectively. The P-12E and closely similar F4B-4 for the US Navy both had the R-1340 Wasp engine, in different marks each rated at 500 hp (373 kW), and possessed top speeds of 189 mph (304 km/h) and 184 mph (296 km/h) at 6,000 ft (1,830 m), the naval fighter's slightly lower speed being attributable to the weight and drag of its specialised deck-landing equipment (arrester-hook) and naval safety gear (dinghy). The ultimate model was the P-12F, of which only a few were built. This had a Wasp rated at 600 hp (448 kW), raising maximum speed by 5 mph (8 km/h). The introduction of a moderately effective system of

supercharging the engine had also led to an increase in service ceiling, that of the P-12E being 28,000 ft (8,535 m), compared with the Siskin IIIA's 27,000 ft (8,230 m), coupled with an improved rate of climb at above 15,000 ft (4,570 m).

Comparable fighter performance was attained by the Curtiss Hawk family, which reached its culmination with the P-6E and F11C for the US Army and US Navy respectively. Both aircraft flew in 1932 and were closely related. But whereas the P-6E was powered by an ethyl-glycol (Prestone)-cooled Curtiss V-1570-23 Conqueror 'C' inline rated at 600 hp (448 kW), the F11C conformed to naval practice in having a 575-hp (429-kW) Wright R-1820-78 Cyclone 9 radial. Both types had neat cantilever main units to their tailwheel landing gear dispositions, with streamlined fairings to reduce drag. The P-6E could carry up to 240 lb (109 kg) of bombs on underwing racks, and

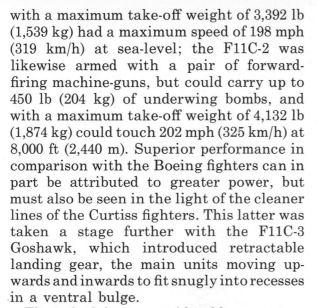

By comparison with the Boeing biplane fighters, the products of the Curtiss company were much sleeker, and finished with a greater care for aerodynamic factors. Illustrated are the Curtiss P-6Es of the 17th Pursuit Squadron, US Army Air Corps, operating from Selfridge Field, Michigan, with a fairly dazzling colour scheme: olive drab fuselage, black and white 'snow owl' markings on the nose and landing gear (mirroring the motif within the fuselage band), chrome yellow flying surfaces, and bright national insignia (those on the upper wings connected by a varying number of spanwise red stripes). The most notable advance in this variant of the Curtiss Hawk series was the adoption of cantilever legs for the main units of the landing gear, which improved the drag factor of the aircraft by a considerable margin.

with a maximum take-off weight of 3,392 lb (1,539 kg) had a maximum speed of 198 mph (319 km/h) at sea-level; the F11C-2 was likewise armed with a pair of forward-firing machine-guns, but could carry up to 450 lb (204 kg) of underwing bombs, and with a maximum take-off weight of 4,132 lb (1,874 kg) could touch 202 mph (325 km/h) at 8,000 ft (2,440 m). Superior performance in comparison with the Boeing fighters can in part be attributed to greater power, but must also be seen in the light of the cleaner lines of the Curtiss fighters. This latter was taken a stage further with the F11C-3 Goshawk, which introduced retractable landing gear, the main units moving upwards and inwards to fit snugly into recesses in a ventral bulge.

There had been considerable argument within the aeronautical world about the advantages and disadvantages of retractable landing gear: on the credit side, all agreed, was a considerable reduction in drag; and on the debit side, all agreed also, there was the additional weight of the retraction mechanism and the extra complexity of the aircraft's 'systems'. Where advocates and opponents disagreed was the ratio between the two factors. Aircraft such as the F11C-3 proved the matter beyond doubt: maximum take-off weight increased by 420 lb (191 kg) and installed power by only 50 hp (37 kW), but maximum speed increased by 23 mph (37 km/h) to 225 mph (362 km/h). Further proof of the retractable landing gear's superiority was given by the Grumman FF-1, which had introduced the feature to the US Navy: with some 600 hp (448 kW) available, this tubby fighter was capable of 201 mph (323 km/h) at 8,000 ft (2,440 m), aided by its clean lines and enclosed cockpit (another bone of contention for fighter pilots) and other streamlined features.

One of the highpoints in the development of the biplane fighter was clearly the Polikarpov I-153 from Russia. This design was originated in 1937 (after the considerably more advanced Polikarpov I-16 monoplane fighter had flown) in the mistaken Russian belief that future combat would see the need for agile biplanes as well as fast monoplanes. The basic wing cellule combined features of the earlier I-15 and I-15bis, with I-type interplane struts and an excellent field of vision for the pilot, added to a more modern fuselage with alloy-tube structure and dural skinning (forward of the cockpit), and retractable main landing gear units. But the extra drag of the biplane configuration meant that even with some 1,000 hp (746 kW), the I-153 was some 50 mph (80 km/h) slower than contemporary monoplanes.

THE END OF THE BIPLANE

There was only so much that designers could do to enhance the performance of biplanes further, for they were faced with inescapable fact that the biplane wing cellule, even with streamlined interplane struts and streamlined bracing wires, was inherently possessed of a high drag factor. Speed, that touchstone of fighter design in the 1920s and 1930s, could indeed be raised, but only by careful and expensive cleaning up of the airframe in other respects, or by enormous increases in the installed power (with consequent problems stemming from the need for stronger and therefore heavier airframes), or by recourse to palliatives such as retractable landing gear dispositions. Such was the entrenched position of the biplane fighter, however, that all these factors were tried, individually or collectively. The designers were faced with an insurmountable problem, however, quite separate from the aerodynamic one: the

ethos of the biplane fighter had not altered significantly since the First World War, so fighter pilots and the senior officers who sanctioned the new aircraft (men who had generally been fighter pilots in the war) called for the same thing time and time again, but with constant improvements in performance. What was required in the early 1930s, therefore, was a First World War fighter (in terms of firepower, agility and control responsiveness) with the more modern attributes (radio, oxygen, improved structure etc) grafted on by the virtue of more powerful engines. It was a vicious circle from which there was no apparent exit so long as the fighter pilots liked to fly by the seats of their pants, with the wind on their faces, in supremely aerobatic, lightly loaded aircraft.

But commercial sense had already cut a wide gap in this vicious circle, though it took the air forces some time to realise it: one of the parameters for success in commercial airline operations, which were well developed by 1930, was, and is, the carriage of maximum payload with minimum fuel consumption. This factor, simple in concept but complex in execution, spurred technological progress towards the advent of big monoplanes of clean line, of cantilever configuration, with a monocoque fuselage and overall stressed-skin construction in light alloy, and with advanced features such as variable-pitch propellers and high-lift devices, supplemented rapidly by de-icing equipment and pressurisation to permit true high-altitude performance. The first civil aircraft to include most of these features was the Boeing Model 247 of 1932, though its features had been presaged in a number of earlier civil and military aircraft which came from Boeing. So far as the military was concerned, the main effect of this revolution in civil aircraft lay in the fact that there was little conceptual difference between the airliner and the bomber: both were designed for the carriage of heavy payloads over substantial ranges, and features of the new airliner breed soon began to appear in

The culmination of the basic type of biplane fighter stemming from the First World War may be regarded as the Bristol Bulldog. This replaced the first generation of British fighters after the First World War (Armstrong Whitworth Siskin and Gloster Gamecock), offering better levels of performance by aerodynamic refinement and greater power rather than by any radical innovation. Seen here are examples of the initial production version, the Bulldog II, which adhered to First World War tenets in its through-axle landing gear, open cockpit, two guns and high-drag biplane wing arrangement, supplemented by more advanced features such as radio equipment and oxygen gear.

THE MONOPLANE COMES OF AGE

Right: A Boeing P-26C 'Peashooter' of the 19th Pursuit Squadron, 18th Pursuit Group, US Army Air Corps, in flight over Hawaii. Boeing's first (and last) successful monoplane fighter, the P-26 was superficially an advanced aircraft, but the monoplane wing was braced to the upper fuselage and spatted landing gear legs, the fixed type of landing gear having been retained for its simplicity and low structure weight.
Below: The Fiat CR.42 may be regarded as the ultimate biplane fighter, first flying in 1939 and resulting from Italy's experience in the Spanish Civil War. Agile and strong, the CR.42 could reach 267 mph (430 km/h) on 840 hp (627 kW), compared with the P-26's 234 mph (377 km/h) on 550 hp (410 kW), but contemporary monoplanes of cantilever construction and fitted with retractable landing gear could surpass 350 mph (563 km/h).

bombers. The lessons were plain to see: the British were pleased to introduce into service in 1931 their first fighter capable of exceeding 200 mph (322 km/h) in level flight (this Hawker Fury I could just touch 205 mph/330 km/h at 13,000 ft/3,960 m); a year later the US Army Air Corps began evaluation of the Martin XB-907A monoplane bomber, which could reach 207 mph (333 km/h) at 6,500 ft (1,980 m). And simple arithmetic will confirm that to avoid the need for fuel- and maintenance-intensive standing patrols, the fighter needs a considerable margin of speed over the bomber to ensure certain interception. To rub salt into the biplane fighter's wounds, it was clear that the biplane fighter was an aircraft of fully developed maturity, whereas the new monoplane bombers were nowhere near their full potential in the early 1930s.

The biplane fighter was dead, but its protagonists refused to admit the facts and the type flew on into a classic senescence with types such as the British Gloster Gladiator (254 mph/409 km/h), the Italian Fiat CR.42 Falco (261 mph/420 km/h), the Russian Polikarpov I-153 (267 mph/430 km/h) with retractable landing gear, and the US Grumman F3F (231 mph/372 km/h).

Already the first monoplane fighters had appeared, but these were intermediate types, combining attributes of their biplane antecedents and true monoplane descendants. The way had been shown in the war by a number of monoplanes that had failed for a variety of reasons (official prejudice, structural problems, arrival too late for combat and the like), including the Bristol M.1C, the Fokker D VIII, the Fokker E types (which are of historical significance as having ushered in the era of the true fighter, thanks to their provision with a synchronised machine-gun able to fire through the disc swept by the propeller), the Junkers D I and the Morane-Saulnier N. Further experiments followed in the 1920s, the French in particular showing a penchant for this type of machine with classics such as the Dewoitine series of parasol-wing monoplanes (D.1, D.9, D.21, D.27 and D.37 series) and other parasol-wing designs from the boards of Gourdou-Leseurre (models B 3 and 32), Morane-Saulnier (model 225) and

Right: The Mitsubishi A5M was the Imperial Japanese Navy's first monoplane fighter, and a classic of its type. Though it retained fixed landing gear and an open cockpit, the 'Claude' – as it was coded by the Allies in the Second World War, had a cantilever wing and metal construction, offering most of the biplane's agility with some of the monoplane's performance.
Below: Early experiments with monoplane fighters, such as this Boeing XP-15 of 1930, often tried to maintain the pilot's field of vision by recourse to expedients such as the parasol configuration. The trouble with such layouts was, of course, that the struts entailed enormous drag and so slowed the aircraft almost as effectively as a second set of wings.

Wibault (model 7). Poland also favoured the high-wing monoplane, her first production fighter to this ideal being the PZL P-7 of 1932. Such parasol- and high-wing configurations offered the pilot an excellent field of vision, but none of the structures was a true cantilever, so the design suffered from a mess of drag-producing struts and wires. Boeing in the USA went a step further in the design of the low-wing P-26, a low-wing fighter introduced in 1933. This was the Americans' first low-wing all-metal fighter (with flaps later in the production run), but it retained a certain quantity of wing-bracing and fixed landing gear in a conscious effort to keep down weight and so enhance performance with the current generation of radial engines. Similar design choices resulted in comparable French and Japanese fighters at a slightly later date:

the Dewoitine D.500 and D.510 for French service, the Mitsubishi A5M for the Imperial Japanese Navy and the Nakajima Ki-27 for the Imperial Japanese Army. But though these French and Japanese designs retained the fixed landing gear, they were (unlike the Boeing design) of cantilever monoplane construction.

By the early 1930s all the ingredients for a radically new type of fighter were available. All that was needed was someone to put them all together in the right way. That someone was the talented Russian designer Nikolai Polikarpov, and his decisive contribution to aviation was the I-16, which first flew in 1933. (It should be noted that another gifted Russian designer, Andrei Tupolev, produced a competing monoplane design, the I-14, that flew a few months earlier but failed to enter service.)

Right: Had the French air force possessed more Dewoitine D.520 fighters when the Germans invaded in May 1940, French defences would have been much more effective, for this small fighter had a considerable punch and was well off in terms of performance and manoeuvrability compared with the Bf 109E.

Below: The blocky appearance that had characterised French aircraft of the 1930s disappeared entirely with the svelte Dewoitine D.520 single-seat fighter. This type, which entered service in 1939, was in most ways comparable with the best British and German fighters.

Left: Few examples of the Dewoitine D.520 survived the Second World War, one being preserved in the Musée de l'Air at Chalais Meudon near Paris.

POLIKARPOV I-16

The I-16 introduced new standards of aerodynamic cleanliness to fighter design, was a low-wing monoplane of metal construction with retractable landing gear, and featured a standard armament of four machine-guns in its true production form. An enclosed cockpit was provided, but pressure from service pilots meant that this was soon removed.

The first definitive version was the I-16 Type 4, which entered service in 1935: powered by a 700-hp (522-kW) M-25 radial, this had a maximum take-off weight of 3,135 lb (1,422 kg) and a top speed of 282 mph (455 km/h). Speed was thus greatly increased over that of contemporary biplanes, and this factor was attributable in part to additional power, in part to clean design, and in part to the type's low power loading. These same factors also gave the I-16 a superior rate of climb, but manoeuvrability was inferior to that of biplane competitors. Additionally, short moment arms and large-area control surfaces made the I-16 tricky to fly even by experienced pilots. As might be expected with such a type, development of the basic airframe was constant, coupled with that of the engine, and the type reached its definitive state with the I-16 Type 24 of 1939: this was powered by the 1,000-hp (746-kW) Shvetsov M-62 radial and weighed in at 4,520 lb (2,050 kg) for take-off. The extra power was combined with aerodynamic improvements, including an enclosed cockpit, to produce a maximum speed of 326 mph (525 km/h) at sea-level; armament improvements had also been continuous, and the I-16 Type 24 led the world in basic firepower and armament flexibility: inbuilt guns comprised two wing-mounted 20-mm ShVAK cannon and two fuselage-mounted 7.62-mm (0.3-in) ShKAS machine-guns, and under the wings could be carried two chemical containers, or six RS-82 rocket projectiles, or six small bombs. Rocket projectiles for aircraft use were a weapon pioneered by the Russians, and with these missiles the I-16 Type 24 was a potent ground-attack platform, as indicated by combat use in that role during the 'Nomon-han Incident' against the Japanese in Manchuria during 1939.

The nett effect of the new configuration and armament was a fighter totally superior to the type it had replaced. Emphasis was now placed on speed, rate of turn, rate of climb and acceleration in the climb and dive rather than on purely dog-fighting agility. This meant that the pilot of the more modern aircraft could wait to enter combat on his own terms, and then break off the combat whenever he chose. Such capability placed greater emphasis on structural strength and armament: strength to survive more intensive combat manoeuvring, and armament to inflict mortal damage within the short firing periods imposed by the new tactics; at the same time structural strength was necessary to support the power of the new generation of engines and the considerably heavier recoil forces of the latest weapons (especially the cannon), and to absorb the combat damage that could be inflicted by the heavy batteries of machine-guns and/or cannon sported by the increasing number of modern fighters to emerge in the middle and late 1930s.

The Polikarpov I-16 suffered the fate of many aviation 'firsts': it was soon outclassed by slightly later aircraft. But the I-16's place in history is assured as the world's first cantilever low-wing monoplane fighter with a retractable landing gear disposition to enter service anywhere in the world.

THE FIGHTER
1939-1961

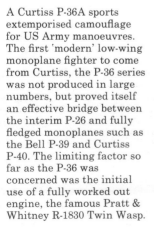

Previous page: While the Polikarpov I-16 can be regarded as the bridge between the biplane and monoplane eras, the Supermarine Spitfire was definitively a classic example of the fully developed monoplane fighter, with an advanced engine, airframe reflecting the contemporary 'state of the art', enclosed cockpit, considerable protection and heavy firepower. Seen here are a pair of Spitfire Vs over the Allied beach-head at Anzio in Italy.

Technically the most important fighter in Italy's armoury in June 1940, the Macchi MC.200 Saetta was a contemporary of the Spitfire, but was a less ambitious aircraft with an open cockpit, relatively low-powered radial engine and indifferent armament. But like other Italian fighters it possessed magnificent agility.

A Curtiss P-36A sports extemporised camouflage for US Army manoeuvres. The first 'modern' low-wing monoplane fighter to come from Curtiss, the P-36 series was not produced in large numbers, but proved itself an effective bridge between the interim P-26 and fully fledged monoplanes such as the Bell P-39 and Curtiss P-40. The limiting factor so far as the P-36 was concerned was the initial use of a fully worked out engine, the famous Pratt & Whitney R-1830 Twin Wasp.

As so often befalls the true pioneer, the I-16 was soon outstripped by marginally later fighters: in this respect it paid the penalty, in concept and in combat, for being the first of its kind, or rather of being the bridge between two eras of fighter. Others that appeared later but still fell into this category were the Curtiss P-36 and Seversky P-35 (both American fighters) and the Morane-Saulnier M.S.406 (the French fighter mainstay at the beginning of the Second World War). None of these aircraft had the intrinsic potential for development into advanced combat aircraft, though the two American machines, it should be noted, formed the design basis for two great fighter series (the Curtiss P-40 and Republic P-47 respectively), while the obsolescent M.S.406 acquitted itself well against the technically superior fighters of the Luftwaffe in 1940. Another fighter that falls almost into this category is the Hawker Hurricane, though the type earned itself an immortal niche in aviation history for its triumph in the Battle of Britain, in which Hurricanes destroyed more German aircraft than all the other British defences combined.

Though good aircraft in their own right, the preceding fighters failed to satisfy at least one of the arbitrary criteria for a 'modern monoplane fighter': the Hurricane and M.S.406 adhered to obsolescent struc-

tural ideas (a boxlike internal structure, albeit built up of light-alloy tubes rather than wood, covered with fabric), while the P-35 and P-36 were structurally more advanced but had only inadequate armament (both aircraft), semi-retractable landing gear (P-36) and the inability to accept radically more powerful engines (both aircraft). In this last respect the designers fell into the trap of using the fully developed form of an existing engine rather than the underdeveloped early version of a new engine with considerable growth potential. In the case of the P-35 and P-36, these engines were the Pratt & Whitney R-1830 Twin Wasp and Wright R-1820 Cyclone respectively, both classic engines dating from the middle 1920s.

Falling rather oddly between the stools of obsolescence and modernity were the Italians, who strove to keep something of the biplane's agility with something of the monoplane's performance, with the result that they procured two fighters possessing the thoroughbred handling characteristics and manoeuvrability of the biplane but without the speed, strength and firepower to tackle monoplanes of the fully developed generation. These two fighters were the Macchi C.200 Saetta and the Fiat G.50, and their one real virtue, shared with the comparable but numerically inferior Regiane Re.2000, was that they possessed the capability for development into genuinely useful fighters when modernised and fitted with more advanced German engines: they thus formed the stock from which evolved the Macchi C.202 Folgore/C.205 Veltro, the Fiat G.55 Centauro and the Reggiane Re.2005 Sagittario.

A contemporary of the P-36, the Seversky P-35 was also built in small numbers and served usefully in introducing US Army Air Corps pilots to the modern monoplane fighter. But like the P-36 it too was limited by its R-1830 radial and wholly inadequate armament.

MESSERSCHMITT BF 109

Thus the first truly modern monoplane fighter was the Messerschmitt Bf 109, a classic aircraft by any criterion, and Germany's fighter mainstay right up to the end of the Second World War with over 35,000 built. The Bf 109's designer, Willi Mes-

serschmitt, was a front runner in structural thinking for aircraft, and was fortunate to have available two engines of great promise: the Daimler-Benz DB 600 and Junkers Jumo 210 inverted-Vee inlines. These were two of the world's new generation of high-powered inline engines, coming after a period in which the radial engine had dominated both civil and military aviation. But now advances in metallurgy, coolant technology and design combined to make the inline engine once again a serious contender, despite its inferior power-to-weight ratio. Moreover, the leanings of designers towards so slim a powerplant for aerodynamically clean fighters appeared to have been confirmed by the overwhelming success of inline engines in the last few Schneider Trophy races, whose float plane contestants had performance and lines quite similar to those of projected fighters. France had never abandoned the inline, having at her disposal the excellent though dated Hispano-Suiza 12Y, but the real impetus to the inline engine renaissance came from Daimler-Benz and Junkers in Germany, from Rolls-Royce in the UK and from Allison in the USA.

In line with contemporary thinking, which envisaged the bomber as the air forces' primary weapon and the fighter as a short-range interceptor of such aircraft, Messerschmitt designed the Bf 109 round a high-powered inline (a Rolls-Royce Kestrel was used in the first prototype, the Jumo 210 in the initial production Bf 109B series, and the definitive DB 600 and its successors from the Bf 109D onwards), a battery of rifle-calibre machine-guns (with provision for later installation of cannon), and only a small fuel capacity. The airframe was tailored as tightly as possible round these components, resulting in a small airframe of high wing-loading, the consequent high landing speed and sluggish handling at low speeds being compensated by large-area trailing-edge flaps and effective leading-edge slots. Standard equipment carried or catered for right from the beginning was oxygen, radio and a reflector gunsight, the last being one of the latest aids to accurate gunnery at high speeds and high g-loadings.

Perhaps the greatest of the first-generation monoplane fighters was the Messerschmitt Bf 109. Willi Messerschmitt had produced the 'ingredients' for this radical aircraft in the preceding Bf 108 Taifun four-seat touring aircraft, but then tailored all the ingredients round the engine, pilot and armament. Seen here is a Bf 109B early production variant with the little-used Junkers Jumo 210 inline and its deep radiator.

Messerschmitt had reasoned well, as the performance of the first definitive Bf 109Ds showed in 1937 and 1938. However, two problems soon began to manifest themselves: the narrow-track landing gear, pivoted in the wing roots to retract outwards into the undersurfaces of the wings, had been dictated by structural considerations associated with the single-spar stressed-skin design of the wing, but proved a serious tactical disadvantage on all but the best-surfaced airfields; and the initial high wing-loading failed to take into account the inevitable increase in this factor as operational experience led to the rapid increase in armament and other weighty items, resulting inevitably in an erosion of combat performance.

Yet there can be no doubt that Messerschmitt had produced a great aircraft, especially when the introduction of the DB 601 in the Bf 109E produced the first version that could stand up well to combat at all altitudes against the best opposition in the world. With its DB 601A developing

1,100 hp (821 kW) at 12,145 ft (3,700 m), the Bf 109E was capable of 354 mph (570 km/h) at 16,405 ft (5,000 m), could climb to 30,100 ft (9,175 m) and had an optimum climb rate of 2,990 ft (910 m) per minute at 13,125 ft (4,000 m). Armament comprised a pair of fuselage-mounted 7.92-mm (0.31-in) MG 17 machine-guns and two wing-mounted 20-mm MG FF cannon, or four machine-guns and one cannon, or four machine-guns. Armour for the pilot was provided, self-sealing fuel tanks reduced the risk of fire, and all in all the Bf 109E was perhaps the best combat fighter in the world, with agility perhaps slightly less than that of the Supermarine Spitfire, but the enormously important ability to dive without a preliminary half-roll thanks to its fuel-injected rather than normally carburetted engine.

One of the main criteria for any aircraft's greatness must be its versatility and ability to accept more power and more load. Here the Bf 109 excelled, for apart from its primary interceptor role, it was also able to undertake, with modifications, the roles of high-altitude interceptor, fighter-bomber, reconnaissance aircraft, ground-attack aircraft, carrier-borne fighter and several others. Power was steadily improved, as was armament, but from the Bf 109G series onwards the type began to suffer from the age of the basic design. Combat capabilities

were indeed improved, but only at the expense of handling characteristics as a result of the increasingly heavy loads that had to be carried.

The ultimate production version of the Bf 109 was the Bf 109K, which was introduced in the summer of 1944. The selected powerplant was the Daimler-Benz DB 605D or L, which delivered some 1,800 hp (1,343 kW) at take-off but was capable of putting out over 2,000 hp (1,492 kW) for short periods when the throttle was 'pushed through the gate' to cut in the automatic methanol-water injection equipment. One of the earlier series' besetting vices had been the heavily framed cockpit glazing, which seriously affected the pilot's field of vision, and on the Bf 109K this was replaced by a 'Galland' hood giving the pilot considerably improved fields of vision. The Bf 109K was evolved specifically to intercept the US day bomber fleets that were tearing the industrial heart out of Germany, and was therefore optimised for high-altitude combat: endurance was a mere 50 minutes, but maximum speed was 451 mph (725 km/h) at 19,685 ft (6,000 m); climb to 32,808 ft (10,000 m) achieved in a mere 6 minutes 42 seconds, and service ceiling 41,010 ft (12,500 m). These figures gave the Bf 109K good performance margins over the B-17s and B-24s of the USAAF, and the inbuilt armament of one 30-mm MK 108 cannon (mounted in the motor to fire through the propeller hub) and two 13-mm (0.51-in) MG 131 machine-guns was more than enough to cause heavy damage. Germany's problem lay in the fact that production of aircraft was not equalled by that of fuel.

The most significant of the early Bf 109s was the 'Emil' or Bf 109E, powered by the great DB 601 inline. This definitive mark had excellent performance, the ability to push straight down into a dive without a preliminary and time-consuming half-roll, and an armament that included both machine-guns and cannon. Though these latter were relatively slow-firing and of low muzzle-velocity (and so limited in range), they did pack a considerably heftier punch than the rifle-calibre machine-guns of British fighters.

Seen at the Confederate Air Force's 'Rebel Field' at Harlingen, Texas, is a Hispano HA-1112 based on the Bf 109 but built in Spain during the early 1950s with a Rolls-Royce Merlin engine (a neat juxtaposition of wartime enemies). The 'German' markings include those of Jagdgeschwader 52 on the nose.

Like the Italians, the Japanese preferred agility to all other factors in the design of their fighters. And while the Japanese offensive was in full spate during 1941 and early 1942, Japanese aircraft reigned supreme in the Pacific theatre, the type acquiring an almost legendary reputation being the Imperial Japanese Navy's Mitsubishi A6M Zero, of the type seen in the two ranks closest to the camera. Adequately armed and with good performance (especially in range), the early A6M2 was later found to have insufficient development potential, structural strength and protection to survive in combat against improved Allied fighters.

Right above: The Ta 152 development of the Focke-Wulf Fw 190D 'long-nose' series appeared too late to enter widespread service, but represents the German peak of piston-engined fighter evolution. Armament was very potent, consisting as it did of one 30-mm MK 103 and four 20-mm MG 151/20 cannon, but performance was also impressive, with a maximum speed of 463 mph (745 km/h) at 33,955 ft (10,350 m) and a service ceiling of 40,350 ft (12,300 m). Had there been more such aircraft, better fuel supplies and skilled pilots, the Ta 152 could have proved a great menace to the USAAF's bombers.
Right below: The Ta 152C was the only variant of Kurt Tank's best fighter to enter service. Powered by a Daimler-Benz DB 603L inline with water-methanol boost, this model is described more fully in the caption above. The type also served as the basis for the Ta 152H with the Jumo 213E/B inline provided with methanol-water and nitrous-oxide boost. Span was increased to 47 ft 5¾in (14.50 m), the combination of power and wing area increasing service ceiling to a prodigious 48,560 ft (14,800 m), maximum speed being 472 mph (760 km/h) at 41,010 ft (12,500 m) with nitrous-oxide boost.

THE OTHER FIGHTERS

The Second World War abounded with fighters of different types, and as the course of the war became increasingly complex, these fighters were forced to double up their roles: few nations could afford the luxury of a defensive interceptor for this purpose alone, so fighters were perforce converted into load-carriers for cameras (reconnaissance machines), bombs and rocket-projectiles (fighter-bombers and ground-attack aircraft) and jettisonable fuel tanks (escort fighters). Worthy, even great, fighters were produced by most of the combatant nations, but anything more than a short resume is unfortunately beyond the scope of this book. Germany's other main single-engine fighter was the classic Focke-Wulf Fw 190, which appeared in combat during 1941. Designed by Kurt Tank, the Fw 190 was designed to provide the Luftwaffe with a more potent, heavier fighter than the lightweight Bf 109. Powered by a 1,760-hp (1,313-kW) BMW 801D radial in its Fw 190A-3 form, the Würger (Butcher bird) was a formidable fighting machine with good armament,

excellent performance, enormous structural strength, and prodigious rates of roll and dive acceleration. Later versions became fearsome ground-attack platforms with enormous loads of disposable ordnance (cannon, bombs and rockets), and the type was later evolved into the 'long-nose' Fw 190D/Ta 152 series with the 2,100-hp (1,567-kW) Junkers Jumo 213 inline, though the installation of an annular radiator meant that the initial versions' radial-engined looks were retained. The definitive Fw 190D-9 of 1944 could touch 435 mph (700 km/h) at 18,700 ft (5,700 m), had a service ceiling of 38,060 ft (11,600 m), could fly 610 miles (980 km) at economical cruising speed, and was armed with two 20-mm cannon and two 13-mm (0.51-in) machine-guns. The special Fw 190D-12 high-altitude interceptor was powered by a 2,050-hp (1,529-kW) Junkers Jumo 213E fitted with MW50 (methanol-water) injection and a three-speed two-stage supercharger, and was capable of 460 mph (740 km/h) at 38,060 ft (11,600 m).

Italy's best fighter of the war was the Macchi C.205 Veltro, evolved from the C.200 by way of the C.202 Folgore. Compared with its immediate predecessor, the C.205 had better performance thanks to the installation of a 1,475-hp (1,100-kW) Daimler-Benz DB 605A, giving a maximum speed

Right: The war which had started so auspiciously for Japan ended in total disaster, epitomised by this scene on the airfield at Atsugi in Japan during September 1945. The graveyard of Japanese aircraft includes (foreground) a Mitsubishi A6M5 Zero with ejector exhaust stubs to provide a small increment in speed, and just behind it a Mitsubishi J2M of the type intended to replace the Zero as an interceptor.

of 399 mph (642 km/h) at 23,620 ft (7,200 m), and an armament of two 20-mm cannon and two 12.7-mm (0.5-in) machine-guns.

The third of the major Axis partners in the Second World War was Japan. Like Italy, Japan had come to the conclusion as a result of combat experience in the 1930s (Italy's experience had been in Abyssinia and Spain, Japan's in China and Manchuria) that the future for fighters lay with lightly loaded and relatively lightly armed aircraft whose strong suit was agility rather than outright performance. But whereas Italy had opted up to a late date for the biplane formula (the Fiat CR.42 biplane had entered service only in 1939) the Japanese had decided on the cantilever monoplane, initially exemplified by the Mitsubishi A5M of 1937 and the Nakajima Ki-27 of 1938 mentioned earlier. Both of these were first-generation cantilever monoplanes with fixed landing gear arrangements, and the technical staffs of the Imperial Navy and the Imperial Army soon came to the conclusion that engines in the 1,000-hp (746-kW) class offered better possibilities than current 700-hp (522-kW) units: performance could be improved by the use of retractable landing gear and variable-pitch propellers, while little of the agility so loved of Japanese pilots would be lost.

There thus emerged two classic fighters, in the form of the Imperial Navy's Mitsubishi A6M Reisen (Zero Fighter) and the Imperial Army's Nakajima Ki-43 Hayabusa (Peregrine Falcon). The A6M entered service in 1940 and the Ki-43 in 1943, and compared with contemporary Western fighters they had adequate performance, exceptional agility and prodigious range (the A6M2 Model 21 had a standard range on internal fuel of 1,265 miles/2,035 km rising to 1,930 miles/3,105 km with the use of

a drop tank). The A6M was armed with two 20-mm cannon and two 7.7-mm (0.303-in) machine-guns, while the Ki-43 was decidedly underarmed with a pair of 7.7-mm (0.303-in) machine-guns. Both fighters were just right for Japan's offensive campaigns of 1941 and 1942, but then their failings were revealed as the Allies went over to the counter-offensive: no growth potential had been built into the aircraft, so they proved generally incapable of accepting more powerful engines, stronger armament and the features (armour protection, self-sealing fuel tanks etc) so necessary in contemporary combat against the steady improvements being made to Allied types.

Improvements were made in the A6M and Ki-43, while newer types such as the Kawasaki Ki-61 Hien (Swallow), Nakajima Ki-44 and Nakajima Ki-84 were introduced to army service. Though these three fighters had their good points, they were plagued by problems of poor workmanship in the airframe and engine, entry into service before aerodynamic problems had been ironed out, and the failings of the Japanese aero engine industry, which had lagged behind the Western nations in terms of its engines' power output. Moreover, the Japanese aero engine industry had almost totally ignored the high-powered inline, and the only inline-engined combat fighter to serve

with the Japanese forces during the war, the Ki-61, was powered by a licence-built Daimler-Benz DB 601. Further Japanese fighters, notably the Mitsubishi J2M and Kawanishi N1K, made their appearance in 1944, but by this time Japanese fighters could not be produced in the quantities necessary to defeat the US strategic campaign against the Japanese home islands. And even if the right fighters had been available in the right quantities, Japan had neither the fuel nor the skilled pilots to deploy the fighters effectively.

The three major Allied powers were the UK, the USA and the USSR, and all three produced great fighters of various types.

Above: The Focke-Wulf Fw 190 was undoubtedly one of the great fighters of all time, and perhaps the finest German fighter to enter widespread service in the Second World War. So versatile was the type that it served in radial- and inline-engined versions, and in a variety of roles from low-level close support to high-altitude interception. Seen here is an Fw 190A-8/U1 tandem-seat conversion trainer, used to allow novice pilots to acquire at least a rudimentary knowledge of the aircraft before taking-off on their first solo flights in the type.

Apart from its basic lines and looks, there was little in common between the original Spitfire I and the penultimate Spitfire 22 illustrated. Powered by the 2,050-hp (1,529-kW) Rolls-Royce Griffon 61 or 85, requiring a five-blade propeller for effective translation of output into propulsive thrust, the Mk 22 was a lively fighter, armed with a quartet of 20-mm Hispano cannon, capable of a maximum speed of 454 mph (731 km/h) at 26,000 ft (7,925 m) and possessing a service ceiling of 43,500 ft (13,805 m). But already this superlative example of the piston-engined fighter had been outmoded by the earliest turbojet-driven fighters, which were considerably faster.

The British mainstays at the beginning of the Second World War were the Hawker Hurricane and Supermarine Spitfire. The Hurricane, of the initial monoplane era, was obsolescent as an interceptor by 1941, but proved an admirable ground-attack fighter with rockets and bombs, and also appeared as a decisive anti-tank aircraft in the North African theatre, in the form of the Hurricane IID with a pair of 40-mm cannon slung under the wings.

The Supermarine Spitfire was in a different category entirely: designed slightly later than the Hurricane, it was of more advanced concept, and remained in production right through the war, acquiring in the process a reputation that remains almost fabulous. In part the Spitfire legend grew because of its extraordinarily elegant, even beautiful, lines; and in part it is derived from the type's ability to remain constantly in the forefront of fighter technology thanks to the basic airframe's ability to accept ever more powerful engines and operational equipment without too great a detrimental effect on handling. Another factor about the Spitfire is that whereas other fighters were pressed with great success into other roles,

the Spitfire remained essentially a dog-fighter: it was used most successfully as a reconnaissance aircraft, and performed creditably in the fighter-bomber role, but will be remembered primarily as the supreme British air-combat fighter of the Second World War, constant updating allowing it to beat all that the enemy could put up in the sky against it.

Designed by Reginald Mitchell, the Spitfire first flew in early 1936 and was soon in production to meet the RAF's requirement for a fast-climbing and agile interceptor. In many respects the Spitfire was akin to the Bf 109, being designed to a similar concept and around the same type of highly promising inline engine, in the British case the Rolls-Royce Merlin. Like the Bf 109 the Spitfire was of all-metal stressed-skin construction, with narrow-track landing gear retracting outwards into the undersurface of the wings. In comparison with the German fighter mainstay, however, the Spitfire had a larger wing, and though flaps were fitted, there was no need for leading-edge slots. Also different was the armament, for the British had decided that cannon were not yet ready for combat use, and instead opted for a battery of no fewer than eight rifle-calibre machine-guns to provide the volume of fire necessary to cripple an opposing bomber in the short time it could be kept in the pilot's reflector gunsight.

The first definitive model of the Spitfire was the Mk IA, which played an important part in the Battle of Britain. This was powered by a 1,030-hp (768-kW) Merlin III, and could reach a maximum speed of 362 mph (583 km/h). As befitted an interceptor fighter designed to work within the British

Supermarine Spitfire Mk IXs of No. 241 Squadron, RAF, patrol round Mt Vesuvius in Italy during the second half of 1943. The Mk IX was a 'stopgap' version of the Spitfire, but was produced in greater numbers than any other mark of this celebrated fighter, for reasons which have never been explained. The Mk IX combined the basic airframe of the Mk V (itself another 'stopgap') and its versatile armament possibilities with an uprated mark of the Merlin engine; the result was a fighter of much enhanced performance, distinguishable from the Mk V mainly by its symmetrical underwing radiators.

radar interception system, the Spitfire IA had only limited range (395 miles/636 km), but had a climb performance inferior to that of the Bf 109E: climb to 20,000 ft (6,095 m) took 9 minutes 24 seconds compared with the Bf 109E's 6 minutes 18 seconds to 19,685 ft (6,000 m), while the Spitfire IA's service ceiling was 1,800 ft (550 m) better at 31,900 ft (9,725 m).

With the end of the Battle of Britain, the Spitfire's range deficiency soon began to reveal itself as RAF Fighter Command went over to the offensive in northern Europe. Other shortcomings revealed by the leap-frog battle of technical and tactical advance were performance shortfalls and armament inadequacies. The range factor could be alleviated only marginally by internal fuel increases, the structure not having been designed with this in mind, so a long-term remedy had to await the remarkably protracted British development of jettisonable external fuel tanks. Spitfire performance increased by leaps and bounds, however, in a series of marks numbering about 30 for Spitfires and five for the equivalent naval version, the Seafire. And along with performance upgradings went improved armament fits and other modifications, the latter intended to keep the Spitfire's handling characteristics up to the latest standards, especially in terms of roll rate and acceleration in the dive, and to improve protective features such as armour and self-sealing fuel tanks.

The need to overtake the Bf 109F led to the introduction in 1941 of the Spitfire V, which was basically the airframe of the Mk II modified to take the Merlin 45, 50, or 55 engine, rated at between 1,415 and 1,585 hp (1,056 and 1,182 kW), and with wings that could accommodate one of three alternative armament fits: eight 0.303-in (7.7-mm) Browning machine-guns, or four Brownings and two 20-mm Hispano cannon, or four Hispanos, though the last was rare. Despite the fact that the Mk V was a 'lash-up', production totalled some 6,460 in versions with standard, clipped or extended wings. The type was also developed into three high-altitude models, the pressurised Mk VI and Mk VII, and the unpressurised but tropicalised Mk VIII. This last is generally considered to mark the high point of the Merlin-engined Spitfire's development, excellent performance being complemented by superlative handling characteristics.

The Spitfire IX was another 'lash-up', introduced in 1942 to give the RAF an answer to the latest German fighters, which outclassed the Mk V by a fair margin. The

Mk VIII was intended for this role, but its development was slow, so the Mk V airframe was modified to accept the Mk VIII's two-stage two-speed supercharged Merlin 60 series engine, rated at between 1,565 and 1,650 hp (1,167 and 1,231 kW). As with the Mk V, three wing spans were possible, and the three armament fits were joined by a fourth, which permitted two 20-mm cannon and two 0.5-in (12.7-mm) Browning machine-guns, plus a maximum bombload of 1,000 lb (454 kg) compared with the Mk V's 500 lb (227 kg). Intended as an interim measure, the Mk IX eventually equipped nearly 100 squadrons, and production was greater than that of any other Spitfire mark, totalling some 5,665 built as such and many more converted from Mk Vs.

Some indication of the Merlin engine's greatness is given by the fact that during its service life power output rose from some 1,000 hp (746 kW) to 1,700 hp (1,268 kW) with an increase in weight of only 210 lb (95 kg). It was appreciated before the war that the Merlin was limited by its capacity of 27 litres (1,648 cu in), however, and it was decided to develop an improved version with similar mounting points but larger swept volume (36.7 litres/2,240 cu in). This emerged as the Rolls-Royce Griffon, initially rated at 1,735 hp (1,294 kW) at a weight of 1,980 lb (898 kg), rising eventually to 2,420 hp (1,805 kW) at a weight of 2,300 lb (1,043 kg).

Various trial installations of the Griffon had been made in Spitfire airframes, and it was decided that the first major production version would be the Spitfire XII, intended as a low-altitude fighter-bomber. However, the major Griffon-engined variant was in fact the Spitfire XIV (957 built), which used the airframe of the Spitfire VIII combined with the 2,035-hp (1,518-kW) Griffon 65 or 66. These models were identifiable by the longer nose (with fairings over the protruding cylinder banks), larger-area vertical tail and, on later models, an all-round vision canopy and cut-down rear fuselage.

The ultimate development of the basic Spitfire resulted in the generally-similar Mks 21, 22 and 24, which entered service just too late for the Second World War. These were powered by the 2,375-hp (1,772-kW) Griffon 61 and could reach 450 mph (724 km/h) at 25,000 ft (7,620 m), and had an armament of four 20-mm cannon. For the first time in the Spitfire's history the wing was revised, and although the basic shape was retained the structure and aerofoil were changed. Final development of the entire family were the superlative land-based Spiteful and carrier-based Seafang, which were built only in very small numbers but were among the fastest piston-engined fighters ever produced.

With the approaching obsolescence of the Hurricane plain to see even before the war, Hawker Aircraft set about the design of a successor, and this appeared in 1941 as the mighty Typhoon, the world's first fighter with a 'bubble' canopy for unimpeded all-round vision. A monstrous aircraft powered by the 2,180-hp (1,626-kW) Napier Sabre II

PZ865 brought to a close an era, as it was the last Hawker Hurricane to be built. One of 4,711 examples of the multi-role Hurricane IIC built by the parent company, it was the 12,780th Hurricane to be produced in the UK, and was delivered in September 1944. By this time the fabric-covered wings of the earlier models had given way to stressed metal skinning, but the Hurricane was definitely of an earlier generation of design, and primitive by late Second World War standards.

Right: From the great Hawker Tempest II (powered by the magnificent Bristol Centaurus radial that was officially frowned upon and therefore failed to enter production and use sufficiently early to play its warranted major part in the Second World War) evolved the Hawker Fury lightweight fighter. This is in itself an interesting notion, for the empty weight of the Fury was greater than the maximum take-off weight of any 1939 single-engined fighter. Nevertheless, the Fury in this form, powered by the Napier Sabre VII, was the fastest Hawker piston-engined fighter, with a maximum speed of some 485 mph (781 km/h). But the whole concept was outmoded by 1946, with jet fighters beginning to dominate the air-combat arena.

inline, the Typhoon suffered from severe structural and engine problems even after being accepted for service, and then proved to have abysmal performance at altitude. But though it failed as an interceptor, the Typhoon then emerged as one of the greatest ground-attack fighters of the Second World War. It was exceptionally fast 'on the deck', could sustain a fair degree of combat damage and still get home, and could carry an effective assault armament: inbuilt guns were a quartet of 20-mm Hispano cannon, and under its wings the Typhoon could carry up to 2,000 lb (907 kg) of bombs or eight devastating 60-lb (27-kg) rocket projectiles. The rocket projectiles gave the aircraft a weight of fire equivalent to the broadside of a light cruiser.

The culmination of Hawker's huge experience with single-seat single-engined fighters, stretching right back to the early 1920s and taking in such classic types as the Fury and Hurricane, was potentially the UK's greatest combat fighter of the war, the Hawker Tempest. This was evolved as a 'thin-wing Typhoon' to have superior performance at altitude. And as if to emphasise the strength-in-depth of the British aero engine industry, the Tempest was produced in two radically different forms: the Tempest II with a 2,500-hp (1,865-kW) Bristol Centaurus radial piston engine, and the Tempest V/VI with the 2,420/2,700-hp (1,805/2,014-kW) Napier Sabre IIB/Sabre VA inline piston engine. Only the Tempest V served in the Second World War, and even this mark was beset by technical problems. However, nothing can conceal the type's versatility as a first-rate interceptor with its four-cannon gun armament, or as a fighter-bomber/ground-attack fighter with its cannon and underwing armament of 2,000 lb (907 kg) of bombs or eight 60-lb (27-kg) rockets. From the Tempest was

Below: It was standard practice in the Second World War to relegate obsolescent fighters to secondary theatres, where they could perform usefully until the enemy sent in some fully up-to-date aircraft. Such a fate befell the Hurricane, which was relegated as a fighter to North Africa, and then became a fighter-bomber in the second half of that campaign and in the Italian campaign.

evolved the lightweight Fury, which failed to enter service, and the Sea Fury naval fighter, which was the UK's last piston-engined fighter to enter service.

Apart from the obsolescent Curtiss P-36 and Seversky P-35, the main fighters in US service before that country's entry into the war during December 1941 were a number of relatively indifferent interim types: the US Army Air Forces' Bell P-39 Airacobra and Curtiss P-40 Warhawk (known for export as the Tomahawk/Kittyhawk series), and the US Navy's Brewster F2A (known for export as the Buffalo) and Grumman F4F Wildcat (known in the UK as the Martlet). In prototype form these fighters had been

nearly equàl to their European counterparts, but the addition of combat equipment and armament (generally inferior to that prevailing in Europe by 1941), coupled with the lack of combat-spurred development, meant that by December 1941 the American fighters had, with the exception of the F4F, fallen behind the latest European standards.

The Bell P-39 was extremely interesting in concept: Larry Bell had seen that great tactical benefit might accrue from the installation of very heavy nose armament (including a 37-mm cannon) if the engine were moved back to a location close to the aircraft's centre of gravity, which would also improve manoeuvrability by a con-

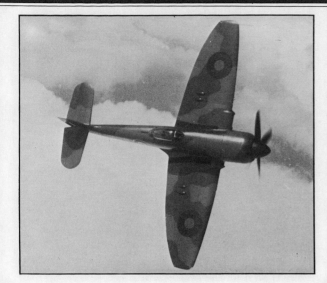

siderable degree. The chosen engine was the Allison V-1710 inline, one of the most significant US engines of the war. Its origins lay in the decision, taken in 1930, for the Allison Division of General Motors to break into the aero engine market, whose high-powered upper reaches were dominated by the radials of Pratt & Whitney and Wright manufacture. Allison therefore decided to develop a new high-output inline engine using the latest techniques. The V-1710 was in every respect a worthy engine, but lacked the design genius of the Merlin/Griffon and DB 601/605 series. The V-1710's main failing was lack of an adequate supercharger, and this restricted its capabilities to the low-

Left: Piston-engined fighters still had a part to play in naval operations after the arrival of the jet, for the earlier powerplant suited it to operations from small decks. Hawker's last such fighter was therefore the phenomenal Sea Fury. *Below:* The Sea Fury FB.60, seen here in British markings, never served with the Royal Air Force or the Fleet Air Arm. The designation was used for 93 single-seat fighters and fighter-bombers delivered to Pakistan.

Right: The Bell Airacobra failed in its intended role as an interceptor, but proved to be a potent low-level attack aircraft, its strength and stability allowing the heavy armament to be used to maximum effect. Seen here are P-39D Airacobras of the USAAF. This variant was developed to provide the type with self-sealing fuel tanks, which combat experience in Europe had shown to be absolutely essential.

Top right: The feature which most distinguished the Bell P-39 Airacobra in the air was its slim nose, made possible by the location of the engine aft of the pilot, from where it drove the propeller by means of an extension shaft. This powerplant configuration had been selected to improve manoeuvrability (by placing the heavy engine nearer the centre of gravity) and to leave the nose clear for a heavy forward-firing armament, including a 37-mm cannon.

Below: An improved progressive development of the P-39, the Bell P-63 Kingcobra failed to find favour with the USAAF, and most of the production run was allocated for export, mostly to the USSR and to France. The former found the type excellent for the ground-attack role.

and medium-altitude brackets, which European experience had shown to be a distinct tactical disadvantage: even if height were not used in combat, it could be traded for speed or vice versa, allowing the better altitude aircraft to dominate the combat. But it was this engine which powered some of the USAAF's most important combat aircraft, notably the P-39 and P-40 already mentioned, and the twin-engined Lockheed P-38 Lightning, and several other designs were emerging round this basic powerplant.

As it was, the P-39 and P-40 found their true places in the combat spectrum as ground-attack fighters: they were immensely sturdy aircraft, steady fliers at low altitude, and good weapons platforms for inbuilt and disposable armament. The P-40 series received a fillip in the P-40F series by the substitution of a Merlin for the V-1710,

but the Warhawk/Kittyhawk type remained firmly committed to the ground-attack role, in which it played a decisive part in the North African and Italian campaigns. The P-39, it should be noted, was one of the first aircraft to use a tricycle landing gear. It was succeeded by the equally capable P-63 Kingcobra, also a notable attack fighter, but one that was built almost exclusively for supply to the Americans' allies, notably the USSR.

The Brewster F2A was essentially an interim type with little flair, and was relegated to training duties after a short and completely disastrous combat career, except in the hands of Finnish air force pilots, who seemed to have had the knack of making even poor fighters perform well against the Russians. But the Grumman F4F was an altogether more significant machine. Shar-

Left: For lack of suitable alternatives, aircraft of the Curtiss P-40 Warhawk series were widely deployed as fighters by the USAAF in 1941 and 1942. But as improved types became available, the Warhawk series began to assume a new significance as a fighter-bomber/ground-attack type.

The Grumman F4F Wildcat was also built at Trenton, New Jersey in the form of the General Motors FM. The body directly responsible was the Eastern Aircraft Division of GMC, and its ultimate version was the FM-2, which was based on the FM-1 (company designation for the F4F built by Eastern), but had improved features such as a lighter airframe, taller vertical tail and more powerful Wright R-1820-56 Cyclone to maintain performance from smaller carriers, particularly the escort carriers that began to be available from 1942. The F4F/FM type was the only dedicated carrier-borne fighter available to the Allies in 1941 and 1942 able to tackle Axis fighters with any real hope of success. The FM-2 illustrated is part of the Confederate Air Force, based on Rebel Field at Harlingen in Texas, and is painted in the livery of VF-41 'The Red Rippers', located aboard USS *Ranger* in 1941.

Below: The F4F-4 was the last Wildcat variant developed by Grumman. It had the typical Grumman features of a tubby fuselage with the main units of the landing gear retracting into its sides below the mid-set wing, and the F4F-4 version introduced folding wings to facilitate stowage aboard increasingly crowded carriers.

undoubtedly was, it was all useful size. The designer was Alexander Kartveli, and he planned the aircraft round the largest available engine, the 2,000-hp (1,492-kW) Pratt & Whitney R-2800 Double Wasp, with a massive turbocharger installation located in the rear fuselage to provide optimum airflow. The rest of the airframe followed this initial logic, with a large wing to support its weight, a big propeller to use its power, a stalky landing gear to keep the propeller from striking the ground, and considerable fuel capacity to keep the engine fed. Armament was also exceptionally heavy, amounting to eight 0.5-in (12.7-mm) Browning machine-guns when the standard US battery was four or six such weapons. When it appeared in service during 1943 the Thunderbolt was undoubtedly fast and long-legged; but it was also too big to dogfight effectively. Nevertheless its range urged its use as an escort for the US bomber fleets beginning to roam over northern Europe, and it was only after the arrival of better escorts that the Thunderbolt found its true metier as perhaps the best ground-

attack fighter of the war: its speed and strength allowed it to avoid or survive flak, while its offensive load of 2,500 lb (1,134 kg) of bombs or ten 5-in (12.7-cm) rockets made it the scourge of Axis transport, fixed defences and troop concentrations. And to an experimental development of the Thunderbolt, the inline-engined XP-47J, goes the distinction of being the world's fastest piston-engined fighter, with a speed of 504 mph (811 km/h), though this speed could have been equalled and perhaps surpassed by the Supermarine Spiteful.

The Russians produced a different type of fighter: their military thinking was geared remorselessly to the superiority of the ground forces, and the air forces were developed as tactical adjuncts to the ground forces. Thus there was little emphasis placed on high-altitude performance, it being sufficient to gain and then keep control of the air at low and medium altitudes. Russian production philosophy also emphasised, then as now, the desirability of keeping lines at maximum production without disruption for the introduction of non-

British use of the monstrous Republic Thunderbolt was confined to the South-East Asia theatre in the Second World War. Here the Thunderbolt I (background), equivalent to the USAAF's P-47B, played a decisive part in the success of ground operations with its eight heavy machine-guns and 2,000 lb (907 kg) of disposable ordnance, including bombs and rockets delivered with such accuracy that they totally devastated Japanese transport, dumps, concentrations and armour.

essential modifications. The result of all this was to provide the air force with large numbers of a few aircraft types, which appeared in only a few major forms whenever a major change proved essential. The approach was thus technologically crude, by Western standards, but supremely suited to the tactical, geographic and climatic conditions prevailing in Russia during the Second World War.

At the time of the German invasion of Russia in June 1941, the Russian air force was equipped with obsolete aircraft: the I-16, for example, was some 100 mph (160 km/h) slower than the Bf 109F, and in every respect an inferior fighting aircraft. But a major re-equipment programme was already under way, and this involved three families of fighter that were to serve admirably throughout the war. The least important of these families was that originating with the design bureau headed by Artem Mikoyan and Mikhail Gurevich. The MiG-1, which entered service in 1940, was powered by the 1,200-hp (895-kW) Mikulin AM-35 inline,

and possessed exceptional performance, with a maximum speed of 391 mph (630 km/h) despite having an open cockpit. This good flight performance was seriously impaired by the type's decidedly tricky handling characteristics, the result of a very short rear fuselage and consequent poor longitudinal stability. In 1941 the MiG-1 was replaced in production by the generally similar MiG-3, which differed principally in having an enclosed cockpit and a 1,350-hp (1,007-kW) AM-35A inline, which raised maximum speed to 407 mph (655 km/h). Both the MiG-1 and the MiG-3 had been designed as high-altitude interceptors, though in common with all other Russian fighters they had provision for underwing stores (bombs, rockets or chemical containers). However, it was in the reconnaissance role that both the MiG fighters made their greatest contribution to the Russian war effort.

Also in the late 1930s, the design bureau headed by Semyon Lavochkin with the technical support of Vladimir Gorbunov and Mikhsil Gudkov evolved a fighter prototype to the same specification as the MiG-1. This initial LaGG-1 was an unusual fighter in that it was built largely of wood at a time when stressed-skin construction in metal had just become the aeronautical norm, and even mixed-construction offerings such as the MiG-1 and Yak-1 (see below) were seemingly dated. But Russia abounds with wood, and workers experienced in this medium abounded in the USSR during the late 1930s. Thus the LaGG-1 had a fuselage built up of plywood skins, impregnated with phenol-formaldehyde, over birch frames, an integral wood fin, and flying surfaces built up over wooden spars and ribs with plywood skinning. Even the engine bearers were of wood. The type entered service in 1940, but only a few examples were built before the LaGG-3 appeared with small improvements, notably to the armament and the powerplant, where the original M-105P engine was replaced by the Klimov M-105PF, whose two-speed supercharger maintained rated power up to higher altitudes. An interesting sidelight into the qualities of the fighter in the early 1940s is given by service evaluation of the LaGG-3 by the Finns and Japanese: the Finns test flew a captured example and considered it indifferent in handling and poor in acceleration; while the Japanese, who had the chance to evaluate an example provided by a Russian defector, thought the Russian fighter too heavy and lacking in agility, with the one saving grace of acceleration in the dive.

The Lavochkin series of fighters really came into its own during 1942 with the appearance of the La-5. This was made possible by the use of a totally different engine, the Shvetsov ASh-82 radial, evolved from the Wright R-2600 Cyclone 14, for which the Russians had secured a licence in the late 1930s. The original La-5, which entered service in October 1942, was powered by the 1,330-hp (992-kW) ASh-82A, and had a maximum speed of 345 mph (555 km/h) at sea-level; though this may seem a relatively low maximum speed, it must be seen in the context of the fighters opposing the La-5, and the Bf 109G-2, for example, could manage only 317 mph (510 km/h) at sea-level. It was only at altitudes of more than 16,405 ft (5,000 m) that the German fighters really came into their own, and Russian fighters rarely ventured over this height. Further development in the Lavochkin fighter series proceeded along established lines: the La-5FN of early 1943 was powered by the 1,640-hp (1,223-kW) ASh-82FN, had a cut-down rear fuselage to improve the pilot's fields of vision, and could reach 404 mph (650 km/h) at 20,995 ft (6,400 m); the La-7 of later 1943 had a 1,775-hp (1,324-kW) ASh-82FN engine and a maximum speed of 413 mph (665 km/h) at 20,995 ft (6,400 m); the La-9 of 1945 with a 1,870-hp (1,395-kW) ASh-82FNV engine and top speed of 429 mph (690 km/h) at 20,505 ft (6,250 m) thanks in part to a smoother all-metal airframe; and the post-war La-11 long-range version of the La-9, with the same engine and maximum speed, but range boosted from 1,078 miles (1,735 km) to 1,584 miles (2,550 km) by the inclusion of extra fuel in place of one of the La-9's four 20-mm ShVAK cannon.

The last of Russia's fighter families in the Second World War was that designed by the bureau of Aleksandr Yakovlev, who started work on a new generation of monoplane fighter in 1938. This first flew in 1940 and entered service in 1941 as the Yak-1. It was the best of Russia's early war fighters, and may be regarded as comparable to the Hurricane I of some five years earlier: the fuselage was of obsolescent mixed construction (steel-tube framework of four longerons, faired out with plywood formers and covered with impregnated plywood skinning), wooden wings and tail surfaces, and fabric-covered metal-framed control surfaces. Power was provided by a 1,100-hp (821-kW) Klimov M-105P, which bore the same relationship to the Hispano-Suiza 12Y as the

Shvetsov ASh-82 to the Wright R-2600. But though in construction the Yak-1 was conceptually akin to the Hurricane, in basic design it was closer to the Bf 109, in that Yakovlev believed that a fighter should be as compact as possible, with a powerful engine allied to a relatively light airframe and heavy armament (in the Yak-1 comprising one 20-mm ShVAK motor cannon and two 7.62-mm (0.3-in) ShKAS machine-guns or one 12.7-mm (0.5-in) Beresin UB machine-gun, plus 500 lb (227 kg) of bombs or six 82-mm (3.22-in) 25-kg (55-lb) rocket projectiles).

From this basic but eminently 'developable' aircraft there sprang a prolific series of fighters in two main streams: one with the same basic airframe as the Yak-1, and the other with a revised structure with metal-sparred wings and the cockpit moved farther aft. In the first stream the Yak-1 was succeeded in 1942 by the Yak-1M, with modifications deemed essential in the light of combat experience. These included the cutting-down of the rear fuselage to allow the installation of an all-round vision canopy, reduction of drag and weight by a reduction of wing span and area, and standardisation on an armament of two 12.7-mm (0.5-in) Beresin UB machine-guns. And in December 1942 a further development in this first stream appeared with the Yak-3, which

was essentially the Yak-1M optimised for high-altitude combat, the Russians having realised that although the decisive air battle might be fought at low and medium altitudes, the high altitudes could not merely be given to the Germans for trouble-free reconnaissance and the like. The Yakovlev bureau at first wanted the more modern Klimov M-107 for the Yak-3, but on Stalin's personal dictate this was refused, the Yak-3 thus appearing with improved versions of the M-105, culminating in the VK-105PF-2 which developed 1,290 hp (962 kW) for take-off. The Yak-3 entered service in mid-1943, and soon built for itself an awesome reputation: at 10,825 ft (3,300 m) the Yak-3 was some 25 mph (40 km/h) faster than the Bf 109G, and at low altitude it could out-turn the Fw 190 with ease. However, at altitudes above 19,685 ft (6,000 m) the German fighters were still superior. Further improvements were effected in the Yak-3U, which finally received the 1,700-hp (1,268-kW) VK-107A and differed from the basic Yak-3 in having an all-metal structure and the impressive armament of one motor-mounted 37-mm cannon and two fuselage-mounted 20-mm cannon. With a maximum speed of 447 mph (720 km/h) at 18,865 ft (5,750 m), the Yak-3U was a formidable fighter right up to the end of the war.

The second development stream of the

The Russian philosophy so far as fighters were concerned was one of simplicity: volume production of only a few variants of the right fighter types, which had to be easy to build and to maintain, have powerful armament, and excel in the low- and medium-altitude arenas considered paramount by the Red Air Force. One of the best examples of this philosophy was the Yakovlev Yak-3, this example being brought to France by the 'Normandie-Niemen' squadron in 1945.

Yak-1 family began with the evolution of the Yak-7 in 1942 as a low-level aircraft more suitable for fighter-bomber than interceptor fighter missions. The immediate origins of this fighter-bomber derivative was the Yak-7V two-seat conversion trainer, which had been followed by the single-seat night-fighter Yak-7A model. From this latter descended the definitive Yak-7B fighter-bomber, still powered by the 1,210-hp (903-kW) VK-105PF but grossing 6,636 lb (3,010 kg) compared with the Yak-1's 6,217 lb (2,820 kg), and with a maximum speed of 339 mph (545 km/h) at sea-level. Armament comprised one 20-mm cannon and one 12.7-mm (0.5-in) machine-gun, supplemented by a disposable load of up to 440 lb (200 kg) of bombs or six rocket projectiles. The Yak-9 was evolved from the Yak-7B late in 1942 by the simple expedient of replacing the wooden wing spars by steel units, the space and weight so saved being used for extra fuel, increasing range from 513 miles (825 km) to 565 miles (910 km). The Yak-9 was itself built in several variants: the basic model with a 1,300-hp (970-kW) VK-105PF-1 or 1,360-hp (1,015-kW) VK-105PF-3 engine and an armament of one 20-mm cannon and one or two 12.7-mm (0.5-in) machine-guns; the Yak-9B fighter-bomber with the same engines, and an armament of three 12.7-mm machine-guns plus up to 1,323 lb (600 kg) of bombs; the Yak-9D escort fighter, evolved from the VK-105PF-3 version of the Yak-9 but with additional fuel capacity; the Yak-9DD longer-range version of the Yak-9D; the Yak-9DK anti-tank fighter with a 45-mm NS-P-45 cannon in the nose; the Yak-9L up-engined prototype with the supercharged VK-105RD engine; the Yak-9P improved version of the Yak-9U interceptor, developed post-war with an all-metal airframe and the 1,650-hp (1,231-kW) VK-107A engine; the Yak-9PVO night-fighter version of the Yak-9; the Yak-9R reconnaissance version of the Yak-9B; the Yak-9T-37 anti-tank fighter with a 37-mm NS-11-P-37 cannon in the nose and provision for special anti-tank bombs; the Yak-9T-45 up-gunned version of the Yak-9T-37 with a 45-mm NS-P-45 cannon in the nose; the Yak-9U improved development of the Yak-9 with an all-metal airframe and 1,650-hp (1,231-kW) VK-107A engine, redesigned canopy and an armament comprising one 23-mm VYa-23V cannon in the nose and two 12.7-mm (0.5-in) Beresin machine-guns; and the Yak-9UF reconnaissance model of the Yak-9U. The significance of this wide-ranging family is attested by its enormous production: some 8,720 Yak-1s, 4,850 Yak-3s, 6,400 Yak-7s and

16,770 Yak-9s, for an overall figure of about 36,740 manufactured.

Though they lacked the sophistication of Allied (and German) piston-engined fighters, by 1944 Russian fighters had reached the point at which they were just as effective in the tactical sense. The aircraft had no frills, but for their designed role of low- and medium-altitude fighter work the Lavochkin and Yakovlev families were perfect. Moreover, they were easy to produce and easy to maintain, and could therefore put in more flight hours per maintenance hour than their Western counterparts.

Classic head-on shot of the North American P-51A Mustang. Designed to a British specification in the course of the Battle of Britain, the Mustang came of age only when engined with the superlative Packard-built Rolls-Royce Merlin. However, engined with the Allison V-1710 (as indicated by the intake above the nose for the down-draught carburettor), the earlier models such as this P-51A were still effective aircraft, even if only at low and medium altitudes.

NORTH AMERICAN P-51 MUSTANG AND VOUGHT F4U CORSAIR

Top left: A crude aircraft by comparison with contemporary Western aircraft, the Yakovlev Yak-1M was nevertheless a highly effective fighter, well suited to the difficult climatic conditions and primitive airfields of the Eastern Front, and of more than holding its own in low-level combat with German fighters. Note the pilot's excellent fields of vision.

Centre left: Counterpart of the Yak-3 (itself a modification of the Yak-1M) from the other branch of the basic Yak-1 series, the Yakovlev Yak-9 was slightly larger and used metal spars in its wing structure. Seen here are Yak-9DD long-range escort fighters, produced specifically for the support of the Yugoslav communist partisans under Tito.

Bottom left: Yakovlev Yak-7B fighters, looking slightly odd in their factory-fresh paint, await delivery to Red Air Force units. This variant was evolved from the Yak-7V two-seat conversion trainer and Yak-7A single-seater, and was distinguishable from the Yak-1 most easily by the position of its radiator, which was moved forward to a position under the front of the cockpit in the Yak-7 series.

In the late 1930s and early 1940s the experience of the previous quarter century with the design, production and service use of piston-engined fighters crystallised in the design of two fighters that must mark the high point of the type: there were, admittedly, fighters that were faster, or more heavily armed, or more agile etc, but none achieved quite the devastating combination of these factors as well as the North American Mustang and the Vought Corsair. The two aircraft thus marked the culmination of the inline, and radial-engined fighter respectively.

The Mustang had its origins in the North American NA-73 design, evolved to meet a British requirement for a high-performance fighter suitable for operations in northern Europe. The design was finalised rapidly in 1940, and the whole process from design initiation to completion of the prototype was achieved in a quite remarkably short time – a mere 117 days. Keys to the Mustang's performance were a relatively large volume, permitting the installation of extensive fuel tankage; a sturdy airframe, well able to accept ever more powerful engines; good manoeuvrability; and cleverly thought-out aerodynamics to keep drag to a minimum. The one 'blot' on the type's early history was the use of the ill-fated Allison V-1710 in early models. This meant that the hoped-for high-altitude performance was not realised, so the type was relegated to army co-

operation and reconnaissance work, where its speed, low-level agility and considerable range allowed the fighter to make full use of its powerful armament.

The Mustang was ordered in fairly large numbers by the RAF and USAAF, but what finally made the design into the war-winner it became was the adoption of the Rolls-Royce Merlin engine in place of the V-1710. The immediate performance improvements are simply illustrated: the Mustang IB with the 1,150-hp (858-kW) V-1710-39 could reach 370 mph (595 km/h) at 15,000 ft (4,570 m), had a best climb rate of 1,980 ft (604 m) per minute at 11,300 ft (3,445 m), and possessed a service ceiling of 30,000 ft (9,145 m); the P-51B Mustang with the 1,450-hp (1,082-kW) Packard-built Merlin V-1650-3 could reach 445 mph (716 km/h) at 30,000 ft (9,145 m), had a best climb rate of 3,320 ft (1,012 m) per minute at 10,000 ft (3,050 m), and possessed a service ceiling of 41,800 ft (12,740 m). Quite apart from the basic improvement in all aspects of aerial performance, the Merlin-engined Mustang also introduced more powerful armament and, most significantly, increased fuel capacity conferred by internal and external tankage. This last meant that at the end of 1943 the USAAF finally received a fighter with the range necessary to escort the heavy bombers to targets deep in Germany. Sluggish on the outward journey when weighed down with this extra weight, the Mustangs could release their tanks at

Bottom: Something of an oddity among the prolific Mustang series was the TP-51D, a two-seater produced only in limited numbers (10 in all, this being the first). These factory examples had full dual controls and a modified cockpit canopy, and other Mustangs were converted to two-seaters in the field.

Bottom: Something of an oddity among the prolific Mustang series was the TP-51D, a two-seater produced only in limited numbers (10 in all, this being the first). These factory examples had full dual controls and a modified cockpit canopy, and other Mustangs were converted to two-seaters in the field.

Below: The most extensively built model of the Mustang was the P-51D, which introduced a one-piece rearward-sliding bubble canopy and, on later models, a small dorsal fin to improve directional stability. A most indistinguishable was the P-51K, which had an Aeroproducts propeller in place of the Hamilton-Standard unit. Production of the P-51D and P-51K was 7,956 and 1,337 respectively.

Bottom: The North American P-51 Mustang has many claims to the title 'best fighter of the Second World War'. Seen here is a prototype P51-D from 1942, with a 360-degree visibility teardrop canopy.

the first sign of opposition deep in Germany, and then reveal their sprightly combat capabilities before returning home on internal fuel: radius of action, with full internal fuel (269 US gal/1,018 litres) and two 150-US gal (568-litre) drop tanks was 1,100 miles (1,770 km). However, what may be regarded as the definitive production version of the Mustang was the P-51D, which was optimised for combat at medium rather than high altitudes (the Germans having lost the ability seriously to contest this latter area by the time of the P-51D's arrival in 1944), and featured an all-round vision canopy to provide the pilot with the best possible field of vision. Performance remained little altered from that of the P-51B, but combat effectiveness was increased by system refinements, additional armament and improved control sensitivity. Wherever the Allied air fleets roamed, there was the Mustang, quelling air opposition for the bomber fleets, supporting the ground forces with its heavy disposable load of bombs and rockets, and disrupting the Axis powers' efforts to move men and matériel by devastating all types of surface transport with machine-gun and rocket fire. The type was further developed as the lightweight P-51H and longer-ranged P-82 Twin Mustang (basically two aircraft joined by a common wing centre section and tailplane), but it was the P-51B and P-51D types that played the dominant part, fully vindicating the Mustang's claim to have been the epitome of the inline-engined fighter. Production totalled 15,469 Mustangs.

Vought's mighty Corsair was an altogether different aircraft, entering service slightly later than the Mustang though its design had been started in 1938. Schemed by Tex Beisel, the F4U Corsair was centred round the use of the most powerful engine currently available, the Pratt & Whitney R-2800 Double Wasp of some 2,000 hp (1,492 kW), to provide the US Navy with a new generation of shipboard fighter with unparalleled performance and versatility. The design was ingenious in the extreme, with a sturdy airframe, considerable internal fuel tankage, inverted gull wings (to reduce overall span and folded height, and to keep

Possibly the greatest fighter of the Second World War, the Vought Corsair was at first banned from carrier-borne operations, but proved a devastating multi-role fighter operating from airfields and airstrips improvised on captured islands throughout the later stages of the Pacific campaign. Seen here are F4U-1D Corsairs of the US Navy on Airfield No. 3 on Iwo Jima, from where they could strike deep into the Japanese home islands. In the background are a B-24 Liberator and B-29 Superfortress, which would have landed here probably as a result of mechanical problems or combat damage.

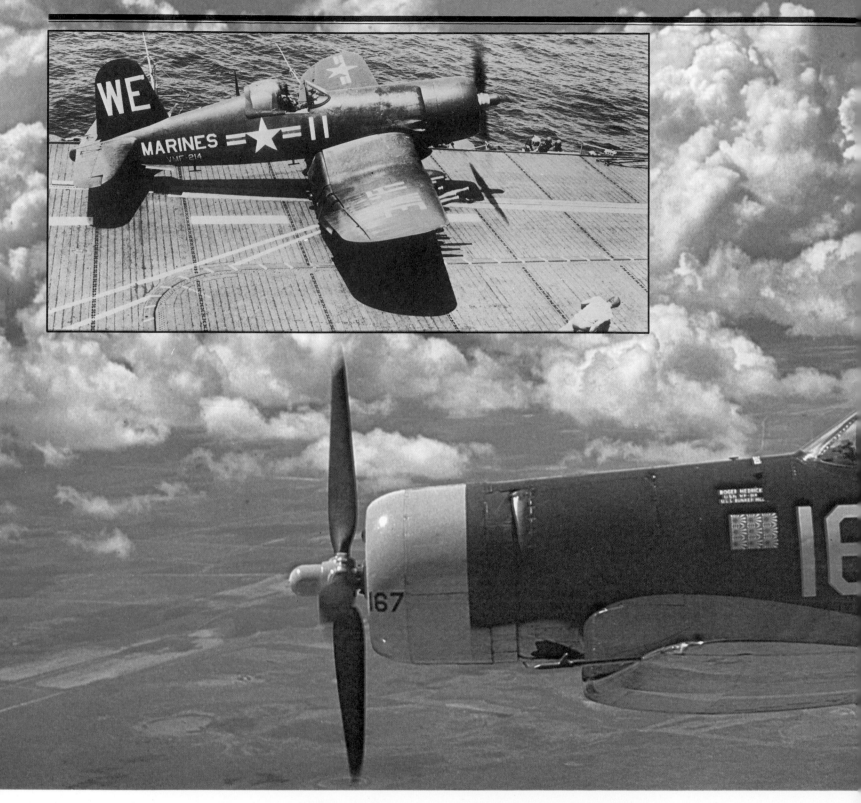

the main landing gear legs short and thus light), and considerable load-carrying capability. Development was protracted by the need for extensive redesign to accommodate extra fuel, but the production F4U-1 entered service late in 1942 as a shore-based fighter, the US Navy having decided that the Corsair's high landing speed and deck-approach characteristics made it unsuitable for carrier operations. However, the Fleet Air Arm introduced the type into carrier service for relatively small ships, and consequently the US Navy reconsidered its earlier decision.

The Corsair could fight it out with enemy fighters (achieving an 11:1 kill:loss ratio in the Pacific), but achieved its greatest successes as a ground-attack fighter. Gun armament was the standard six 0.5-in (12.7-mm) Browning machine-guns or four 20-mm cannon, and underwing loads could comprise bombs, rockets or extra fuel. In any event the Corsair possessed commendable range, suiting it admirably for operations in the Pacific theatre. The type reached its apogee with the F4U-4, powered by the 2,450-hp (1,828-kW) R-2800-18W radial, bestowing a maximum speed of 446 mph (717

km/h) at 25,000 ft (7,620 m). Armament comprised six 0.5-in (12.7-mm) machine-guns with 400 rounds per gun, plus two 1,000-lb (454-kg) bombs or eight 5-in (12.7-cm) rockets. Facts and figures can do little to convey the significance of this great warplane, which remained in production until 1953, with production reaching 12,571 of all marks. In common with the P-51 Mustang (by then redesignated F-51), the Corsair played an important part in the air operations of the Korean War, its low-level manoeuvrability and offensive load making it one of the best ground-attack machines.

Above: The Vought F4U Corsair was another truly great fighter of the Second World War. It was a massive machine of totally distinct appearance, and was equally at home in combat with Japanese fighters or supporting ground troops with guns, rockets and bombs.

Inset top: Once the US Navy had accepted that the Vought Corsair could be operated safely from carriers, the type's operational use and flexibility increased considerably, with the result that ground forces in the later stages of the Pacific war received even better support from this truly great fighter-bomber. Seen here is an F4U-4 of VMF-214, preparing for take-off with its flaps lowered.

THE NIGHT FIGHTERS

An aspect of fighter operations evolved as a practical proposition during the Second World War was night-fighting. Even during the First World War bombers had been used at night in an effort to reduce losses to fighters, despite the fact that navigational accuracy, and hence bombing accuracy, was reduced quite drastically. The lessons of bomber losses to first-rate fighter opposition were largely forgotten in the inter-war years, and both the British and Germans had to relearn them the hard way in 1939 and 1940. The real impetus towards night bombing came with the Luftwaffe's night Blitz of 1940 and 1941 against London and other cities in the UK: with the aid of skilled pathfinder crews and radio navigation aids, the Germans began to exact a heavy toll of British civilians, a toll beyond the capability of the army's AA guns to lessen. The answer, as is so often the case, lay with technology, in the form of airborne radar sets that could with luck and with operator skill 'see' hostile bombers. But despite recent improvements that allowed the production of smaller and lighter radar equipment, these were still quite bulky and heavy. The initial night-fighters were therefore converted light bombers (Bristol Blenheims) and two-seat fighters (the ill-fated turret-armed Boulton Paul Defiant, which made an effective interim night-fighter after a disastrous day-fighter career). But the first effective night-fighter was the massive Bristol Beaufighter twin-engined monoplane, soon supplemented and eventually replaced by the great de Havilland Mosquito, perhaps after the Junkers Ju 88 the most versatile warplane the world has yet seen. The Beaufighter was useful as a night-fighter, but lacked the speed to make difficult interceptions, and eventually found its true place as a strike aircraft.

The Mosquito makes several appearances as a warplane. Designed as a fast and unarmed bomber, it was designed with a wooden airframe (mainly balsa and plywood) of elegant and clean lines, with a powerplant of two increasingly ubiquitous Merlin engines. Such was the performance and agility of the prototypes (one being barrel-rooled with one engine stopped) that the type was rushed into production not only as a bomber but also as a fighter (both day and night) and as a reconnaissance machine. The initial night-fighter version was the Mosquito NF.II, capable of 370 mph (595 km/h) at 5,500 ft (1,675 m) on the power of two 1,460-hp (1,089-kW) Merlin 21s or Merlin 23s, its fighting role being assured by provision of Airborne Interception Mk IV radar (arrowhead antennae on the nose and other antennae on the wings) and an armament of four 20-mm Hispano cannon and four 0.303-in (7.7-mm) machine-guns. Development of this powerful night-fighting platform continued throughout the war, culminating in the much enhanced Mosquito NF.30, a higher-altitude version of the Mosquito NF.XIX. The Mosquito NF.30 was powered by a pair of 1,710-hp (1,276-kW) Merlin 76 inlines, and was capable of 407 mph (655 km/h) at 28,000 ft (8,535 m). Armament had been standardised on a quartet of 20-mm cannon, but much improved operational capability had been bestowed by the use of the excellent SCR-720 radar of

American origins, known to the British as AI Mk X. This set operated on centimetric wavelengths, bestowing much greater clarity of picture and better range, and its antenna was located in a bulged nose without protruding, drag-producing aerials.

A comparable development history was followed by the Germans in their efforts to evolve night-fighters able to inflict mortal wounds on the streams of RAF heavy bombers inflicting increasingly devastating damage on Germany's cities with the nocturnal raids of 1943 to 1945. The first experiments started in 1940 with converted Messerschmitt Bf 110 heavy fighters. The Bf 110 had been designed as a long-range bomber destroyer, but placed into service by the Luftwaffe merely as a heavy fighter, in which role its armament of two 20-mm cannon and five 7.92-mm (0.31-in) machine-guns, one of them located flexibly in the rear of the long cockpit for rearward defence, was expected to confer decisive advantages. But the Bf 110 had proved a poor daylight operator in opposition to single-seat fighters, for it could not manoeuvre with the more agile smaller aircraft. But as a night-fighter the Bf 110 began to

The world's first truly successful night-fighter was the Bristol Beaufighter, which combined the performance, armament and two-man crew needed to use the somewhat primitive radar of the day and still catch the detected aircraft with a fair degree of certainty. Seen here is a Beaufighter IIF, the version powered by Rolls-Royce Merlin inlines instead of the more usual Bristol Hercules radials. This model also introduced dihedral on the tailplane to improve directional stability. The aerials for the AI Mk IV radar were fitted on the fuselage nose and to the outer wing panels.

Below: Germany had as the best airframe basis for its night-fighter development programme the ubiquitous Junkers Ju 88. The nocturnal version reached a powerful peak with the Ju 88G-6b variant: this was powered by two BMW 801G radials, the radar equipment comprised FuG-220 Lichtenstein SN-2 with aerials in high-drag locations on the nose and the wings (reducing maximum speed by some 25 mph/40 km/h), and armament consisted of forward-firing cannon in a belly pack and two more 20-mm cannon in the obliquely-firing *shräge Musik* installation in the fuselage aft of the cockpit.
Right: The Messerschmitt Bf 110G-4 was the first variant of this *Zerstörer* (destroyer) sub-model to appear as a night-fighter, with FuG 212 Lichtenstein radar and an armament of four machine-guns and two 20-mm cannon.

come into its own, for it was quite fast, its size enabled it to carry contemporary radar equipment, and its heavy armament was important for the relatively fleet firing opportunities that presented themselves in night engagements.

The Bf 110 underwent a bewildering number of modifications in the night-fighter role, these centring on the powerplant, armament and radar. Performance was steadily improved (though always beset by the high-drag external antennae of German radar equipment), armament in the Bf 110G-4 variant came to comprise four 7.92-mm (0.31-in) MG 17 machine-guns complemented by two 20-mm MG 151/20 or 30-mm MK 108 cannon (an interesting experiment had been the so-called *schräge Musik* installation of two cannon mounted in the rear fuselage to fire obliquely upwards and forwards), and radar fits could include one of several advanced systems.

Like the British, the Germans also turned

to bombers as the basis of night-fighters, notably the Dornier Do 217 and the Ju 88 mentioned earlier. The former was used in only small quantities, as its performance was strictly limited: the two main models, each armed with four forward-firing cannon and four forward-firing machine-guns, were the Do 217J powered by BMW 801 radials and the Do 217N powered by Daimler-Benz DB 603 inlines. But the Ju 88 was an altogether more formidable aircraft, and without doubt the world's most versatile warplane. Developed as a bomber, with limited dive-bombing capability, the Ju 88A was soon revealed as a potent fighting aircraft with much the same potentials as the later Mosquito. The pressing need for a high-performance night-fighter was felt in late 1940, and the Ju 88 was the obvious candidate for the task. Compared with the Ju 88 bomber variants the fighters were fitted with a 'solid' nose for the radar equipment and forward-firing weapons, in the Ju 88C-6

of 1942 amounting to three 20-mm cannon and three 7.92-mm (0.31-in) machine-guns, supplemented by a *shräge Musik* installation of two 20-mm cannon in some aircraft. Further development led to the Ju 88R series with BMW 801 radial engines, and the Ju 88G definitive version with Junkers Jumo inline engines. This latter version reached its peak with the Ju 88G-7 model, which had FuG 220 Lichtenstein SN-2, FuG 228 Lichtenstein SN-3 or FuG 218 Neptun VR radar in a low-drag nose installation with a pointed plywood nose cone. The Ju 88G-7b could reach 363 mph (585 km/h) at 33,465 ft (10,200 m) on the power of its two 1,725-hp (1,287-kW) Jumo 213E inlines, and was armed with a primary battery of four 20-mm MG 151/20 cannon in a ventral tray, and two similar weapons in a *shräge Musik* installation. Though plagued by technical and political problems, the Heinkel He 219 was Germany's first night-fighter designed as such, and in most respects Germany's best night-fighter, on a par with the redoubtable Mosquito, whose night intruder missions a *Gruppe* of He 219s was formed to counter. Armament was devastating: two forward-firing 20-mm cannon, two 30-mm forward-firing MK 108 cannon, and two MK 108 cannon in a *shräge Musik* unit for the He 219A-5/R2 version.

239515

The Americans, with little chance of German or Japanese bombers attacking their homeland, and with few nocturnal operations requiring the support of night-fighters or night intruders, were late into the development of such aircraft. But it was clear that American forces recrossing the Pacific towards Japan would be vulnerable to nocturnal raids, and so a specification was issued for a long-range night fighter, which became hardware in the form of the powerful Northrop P-61 Black Widow. This was conceptually similar to the Lockheed Lightning in design, but was considerably larger (to house a three-man crew, radar and exceptionally heavy armament) and powered by a pair of 2,000-hp (1,492-kW) Pratt & Whitney R-2800-10 Double Wasp radials. An interesting armament configuration was chosen: four fixed forward-firing cannon, and four 0.5-in (12.7-mm) machine-guns

in a remotely controlled turret above the central nacelle. The Black Widow was in every respect an impressive fighter, with a maximum take-off weight of some 28,500 lb (12,928 kg) but considerable agility thanks to the provision of full-span trailing-edge flaps, the usual ailerons being replaced by spoilers. With its performance, agility and firepower the P-61 was soon used as a bomber destroyer in Europe, and was highly prized as an intruder as the fixed armament could be supplemented by four 1,600-lb (726-kg) bombs carried under the wings.

Italy, Japan, and the USSR lacked the electronics industries to develop effective radar, and thus failed to produce night-fighters in the sense accepted in the West, though Japan did evolve a number of heavily armed twin-engined fighters designed to combat the American bomber fleets pounding the home islands in 1944 and 1945.

Above: The Northrop P-61 Black Widow was the Second World War's nocturnal operator *par excellence.* It was a massive aircraft for its type, but provision of two powerful engines ensured high performance, and manoeuvrability was excellent. Radar was the classic SCR-720, gun armament was four 20-mm cannon (and four 0.5-in/ 12.7-mm in a dorsal turret in some models), while four 1,600-lb (726-lb) bombs could also be carried.
Left: A daintier solution was the Lockheed P-38M, evolved from the P-38L single-seater by adding a second seat (for the radar operator) behind the pilot, and by adding radar in a pod below the nose.

THE ADVENT OF THE JET ENGINE

Not surprisingly, the piston-engined fighter reached a peak of development in the Second World War, largely as a result of the innovative thinking of the late 1930s and the tactical spur of the war itself. But this peak was to be short-lived, for the piston engine had been rendered obsolescent, both in the UK and in Germany, by the advent of the gas turbine engine just before the outbreak of war. It was soon realised that even these rudimentary turbine engines were a power-plant to be considered seriously as primary motive power for high performance aircraft. It had to be admitted, of course, that there were serious problems to be overcome: the engines ran at very high temperatures and speeds, causing the designers severe head-aches with metallurgical aspects of their engines, and fuel consumption was prodigiously heavy. But on the other side of the coin the jet engine was relatively uncomplicated compared with the piston engine, clearly had great development potential, was notably free of the vibration factors associated with reciprocating machinery,

had an admirably high power-to-weight ratio, and had the distinct advantage of producing its power in a form that could be used directly as thrust, without the weight, complexity, torque and aerodynamic considerations of the piston engine, which was now severely limited by problems resulting from the propeller blades travelling at close to the speed of sound and so running into compressibility troubles.

Both sides were fairly swift in introducing jet-powered aircraft during the Second World War: the Germans had the Arada Ar 234 reconnaissance bomber and the Messerschmitt Me 262 fighter, and the British the Gloster Meteor fighter. Other types, which failed to enter service, were the German Heinkel He 162 fighter, the British de Havilland Vampire fighter, the American Bell P-59 Airacomet fighter and the Lockheed P-80 Shooting Star fighter. Other designs were evolved, several of the Allied types serving as interim combat aircraft pending the development of aircraft that could take full advantage of the turbojet powerplant. Thus what is most readily noticeable about these interim types is that they were really piston-engined concepts 'translated' into jet-engined hardware: the airframes differed little from those of 'con-

The Messerschmitt Me 262 was a true portent of fighter developments in the later 1940s and early 1950s thanks to its advanced aerodynamics, jet engines and tricycle landing gear. This is an Me 262B-1a/U1 night-fighter.

Top right: One of the many forms into which the Meteor was developed was the night-fighter, and seen here is an example of the Meteor NF.12, built by Armstrong Whitworth which was responsible for the design and construction of all night-fighter Meteor variants. This particular mark combined the wings of the Mk III with the tail unit of the F.8, while the need to locate the radar in a nose radome meant that the armament of four 20-mm cannon had to be moved out into the wings. The first Meteor NF.12 flew in 1953, but by this time the night-fighter was nearing the end of its time as a useful type: subsequent developments concentrated on clear-weather and all-weather aircraft, the latter able to operate at night.

Centre right: The last single-seat variant of the Lockheed Shooting Star series was the P-80C, which appeared in 1948. This had the six-gun armament of the F-80a, but introduced the ability to carry two 1,000-lb (454-kg) bombs or 10 5-in (127-mm) rockets.

Bottom right: Entering service slightly later than the Gloster Meteor, the Messerschmitt Me 262 may truly be regarded as the first real jet fighter. It was conceptually more advanced than the Meteor, and carried a more powerful armament: four 30-mm MK 108 cannon in the nose, while some models had provision for up to 24 55-mm (2.17-in) R4M unguided air-to-air rockets under the wings.

Above: The Gloster Meteor was the world's first jet fighter, and though not as advanced conceptually as the Me 262, stayed in production until the 1950s in a wide variety of marks. Seen here are Meteor F.3s of No. 56 Squadron, RAF.

Far left: The Bell P-59 Airacomet was the USA's first jet fighter, but was not a success and underwent little development other than for trials purposes.

ventional' aircraft except where the power-plant dictated to the contrary, and performance was boosted considerably, but not as much as the engines' potential should have dictated.

The most important in the interim gaggle of aircraft was the Messerschmitt Me 262, not so much for itself, but for the fact that it was close to the cutting edge of German technological and aerodynamic thinking, which was the first to come to grips with transonic flight and its control difficulties: at speeds of about that of sound, the air flowing round any body is compressed and becomes turbulent, requiring special design and construction techniques to secure a safe break through to the calmer air on the other side of the 'sound barrier'. The most important of the design considerations appreciated by German research was the advantage of swept flying surfaces to delay the onset of compressibility problems. This research became available to the Allies in 1945, and soon swept-wing aircraft began to appear over the skies of France, the UK, the USA and the USSR. Many of these were pure research aircraft, some of them were powered by thrusting but unreliable rocket engines in the manner of Germany's extraordinary Messerschmitt Me 163 flying-wing fighter of the Second World War, and several of them were unmitigated failures that cost the lives of their gallant test pilots.

The Lockheed P-80 Shooting
Star was potentially the best
fighter of the Second World
War, but appeared too late
to make all but the most
fleeting appearance. After
the war, however, it was
widely produced as the F-80
series of fighters and
fighter-bombers, the RF-80
family of reconnaissance
aircraft, and the prolific and
long-lived T-33 trainer type.

THE NORTH AMERICAN F-86 SABRE AND MIKOYAN-GUREVICH MiG-15

By the late 1940s there began to appear swept-wing combat aircraft, and in the fighter field the two most important were the North American F-86 Sabre and the Mikoyan-Gurevich MiG-15, which history pitched into battle over the unlikely and inhospitable terrain of Korea. These two fighters represented the first definitive step into the true age of the jet-powered fighter, and were formidable warplanes. Both aircraft also made full use of the German research that became available in 1945, and emerged as moderately swept designs with certain points of commonality: a straight-through design for the powerplant, with the inlet in the nose and the jetpipe terminating under the tail, lack of sophisticated radar, standardised gun armaments (one 37- and two 23-mm cannon in the MiG-15, and six 0.5-in/12.7-mm machine-guns in the Sabre). However, the MiG-15, which first flew in 1947, had an all-moving powered tailplane set two-thirds of the way up the broad-chord vertical tail, and this proved a decided advantage in ensuring adequate longitudinal control at transonic speeds. The Sabre was undoubtedly a better-made fighter, but suffered at first from lack of a powered elevator, though such a unit was provided on the F-86E from 1950 onwards.

When the MiG-15 and F-86A joined combat over Korea from December 1950, it was clear that in some respects the MiG-15 was superior to the American fighter. Extensive evaluation of combat reports revealed, however, that the MiG-15 was somewhat prone to compressibility problems at high subsonic speeds, and that it tended to snap into a spin from very tight turns. But what gave the Americans a decisive advantage over the MiG-15 pilots was their altogether superior training, combined with the availability of

The Mikoyan-Gurevich MiG-15 came as a very considerable shock to the Western nations, who had prided themselves on their technological superiority to the Russians. But though the MiG-15 used developed versions of the British Rolls-Royce Nene engine, there can be little doubting of the Russians' enormous achievement in producing this great air-combat fighter, which is still in fairly widespread service in the 1980s in the MiG-15 UTI trainer version illustrated.

Far left: The F-86D 'Sabre-Dog' was the all-weather interceptor version of the North American Sabre. It first flew in prototype form in 1949, and featured a revised nose to accommodate radar above the inlet, and the replacement of the guns as primary armament by an extendable underfuselage tray carrying 24 2.75-in (69.85-mm) unguided rockets. Most F-86Ds were later upgraded to F-86L standard with wings of greater span and revised avionics and electronics.

Left: The Korean War had shown with indisputable clarity that British fighters were obsolete in the early 1950s. The new swept-wing Hawker Hunter was under development, but until this was available in adequate numbers the RAF was put in the embarrassing position of having to use imported aircraft, in the form of 430 Canadair-built F-86E Sabre Mk 2 fighters. This model was the first fitted with the all-moving tailplane.

Aesthetically satisfying and militarily potent, the North American F-86 series brought new standards of combat performance into service. Clearly visible are the very clean lines, excellent fields of vision from the bubble canopy, fuselage-mounted gun armament and small inlet bulge for the ranging radar.

From the straight-wing Grumman F9F-5 Panther, the company was able in 1951 swiftly to develop the swept-wing F9F-6 Cougar. With only an extra 1,000-lb (454-kg) of thrust, the Cougar had a maximum speed of 690 mph (1,110 km/h) at sea-level compared with the Panther's 579 mph (932 km/h) at 5,000 ft (1,525 m), eloquent testimony of the superiority of swept surfaces at high subsonic speeds.

a primitive radar gunsight.

The pace of operations in Korea proved a great spur to development of these two basic fighter families, the Communists receiving the improved MiG-15bis in 1952 and the Americans the much superior and more manoeuvrable F-86F at the end of the same year. Compared with the MiG-15, the later model had an uprated powerplant (6,990-lb/3,170-kg water-injection thrust VK-1A turbojet in place of 5,456-lb/2,475-kg thrust RD-45FA), revised airbrakes and perforated area-increasing flaps; the F-86F

had a revised wing, and power provided by a 5,970-lb (2,708-kg) thrust General Electric J47-27 turbojet. The extra power and manoeuvrability of the F-86F gave it a decided advantage over the MiG-15bis.

The limiting factor in further development of the MiG-15 series was the use of a single centrifugal-flown turbojet, the RD-45/VK-1 series evolved from the British Rolls-Royce Nene. This imposed restrictions on the designer, who was forced to adopt a large-diameter fuselage. The F-86 was powered by the axial-flow General Electric J47 and

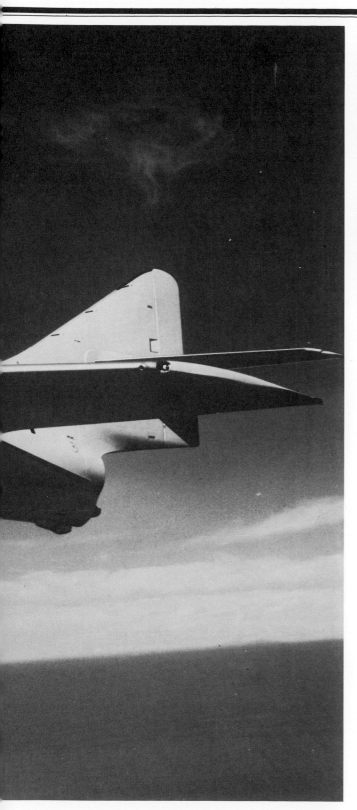

modified to accommodate the 7,500-lb (3,402-kg) thrust Rolls-Royce Avon R.A.7 turbojet and a gun armament of two 30-mm Aden cannon. In the definitive Mk 32 model, the Avon-Sabre could also carry two AIM-9 Sidewinder air-to-air missiles, the up-and-coming weapon of the 1950s, supplemented by 2,000 lb (907 kg) of bombs or 24 3-in (7.62-cm) rocket projectiles. The American peak was reached with the F-86L, derived from the all-weather F-86D which introduced effective nose radar for airborne search and tracking, a large quantity of automatic flight control systems to leave the pilot free for his primary task, and an armament of 24 $2\frac{3}{4}$-in (6.99-cm) Folding-Fin Aircraft Rockets, unguided weapons carried in a box within the lower fuselage, the box being extended into the airflow for automatic firing dictated by the radar and primitive onboard computer. This 'Sabre Dog' may be regarded as the most important stepping stone towards the next generation of fighter aircraft.

Fighters of the same generation as the MiG-15 and F-86 were not in the same class of excellence, but some are nevertheless worthy of mention: the Republic F-84 Thunderjet of 1947, a straight-wing multi-role American design that was transformed into a powerful fighter-bomber as the swept-wing F-84F Thunderstreak, which was a mainstay of NATO's European partners and able to carry nuclear weapons; the McDonnell F2H Banshee for the US Navy, developed from the FH Phantom of late-World War II; the Grumman F9F Panther for the US Navy, with straight wings and a centrifugal-flow powerplant; updated versions of the Gloster Meteor and de Havilland Vampire for the British services and for export; the Lockheed F-94 Starfire developed for the USAF as a derivative of the F-80 Shooting Star

In the UK, de Havilland still concentrated its efforts on aircraft with good performance but aerodynamic and structural simplicity. With the coming of the jet age, performance began to suffer, and the Vampire NF.10 night-fighter of 1951 had a maximum speed of only 550 mph (885 km/h) at 20,000 ft (6,095 m) on the restricted power of its 3,350-lb (1,520-kg) thrust de Havilland Goblin 3 turbojet.

improved J73 engines with considerably greater development potential. Thus when the Russians were forced to turn to different designs to try to keep a qualitative edge over the Americans, the F-86 proved capable of useful development and service right through the 1950s. Models were evolved as potent fighter-bombers, but perhaps the ultimate expression of the Sabre philosophy was achieved with a non-American version, the Australian-built Commonwealth Aircraft Corporation Avon-Sabre. Based on the F-86F, the Avon-Sabre was extensively

The Lockheed F-94 Starfire took the evolution of the jet fighter a step further than the F-80 Shooting Star. For whereas the F-80 was a first-generation clear-weather interceptor, the F-94 was a second-generation all-weather fighter, its extra capabilities being made possible by the carriage of a second crew member to use the new radar equipment provided for all-weather operations. Early Starfires had a conventional nose-mounted armament of machine-guns, but the F-94C variant illustrated went slightly further into the future, with a primary missile armament, though the missiles used were unguided: 2.75-in (69.85-mm) Folding-Fin Air Rockets, of which 48 were carried (24 in a ring round the radome, faired by retractable shields, and the other 24 in two wingtip pods). Production began in 1949.

Bottom left: From the straight-wing F-84 Thunderjet, Republic evolved the more potent F-84F Thunderstreak by adding swept flying surfaces. The prototype flew in 1950, and during the early 1950s the USAF and America's more important allies were receiving a fighter-bomber of markedly improved performance, able to carry up to 6,000 lb (2,722 kg) of disposable stores.

Bottom right: Roughly a contemporary of the US Thunderstreak, the de Havilland Vampire FB.5 fighter-bomber first flew in 1949, and marked the retirement of the Vampire from a primary role of interception to that of close support for ground forces. Wing span was cut by 2 ft (0.61 m), and while the gun armament of four 20-mm Hispano cannon was retained, provision was also made for the carriage of 2,000 lb (907 kg) of bombs or rockets under the wings.

with 48 unguided rockets and radar in the nose; the Swedish Saab J29 pod-and-boom design with swept flying surfaces; the Northrop F-89 Scorpion all-weather interceptor for the USAF; the Grumman F9F-6 Cougar swept-wing modification of the Panther for the US Navy; the de Havilland Venom multi-role fighter based conceptually on the Vampire; the Avro Canada CF-100 Canuck all-weather fighter; and, most importantly, the superb Hawker Hunter, which was perhaps the culmination of the subsonic fighter generation in much the same way as the Tempest and Sea Fury from the same stable were the ultimate piston-engined fighters, and the Mikoyan-Gurevich MiG-17, which can to a certain extent be considered the Russian equivalent of the Hunter.

Below: The Saab 29A Tunnan was a remarkable achievement for the small Swedish aircraft industry.

Right: Designed to provide the Royal Canadian Air Force with an effective all-weather fighter for use in Canada's particular climatic and geographical conditions. Gun armament was located in a ventral tray, leaving the nose clear for radar, while additional armament was carried in the wingtip pods, in the form of 58 unguided rockets. The aircraft illustrated is the CF-100, a later modification designed for electronic countermeasures.

Below: The Northrop F-89 Scorpion was a true pioneer, and the USAF's first multi-seat all-weather interceptor. Seen here is an F-89A, of which deliveries began in 1950. Radar was housed in the nose, and the armament comprised six 20-mm cannon, which was particularly heavy for a USAF fighter of the time. Later models had a primary armament of 52 folding-fin unguided rockets in wingtip pods, or alternatively two GAR-1 Flacon guided missiles when these became operational.

THE NORTH AMERICAN F-100 SUPER SABRE AND MIKOYAN-GUREVICH MiG-19

Supersonic performance was introduced to fighters by the same two teams that had produced the F-86 Sabre and the MiG-15. The F-100 Super Sabre started life as a design exercise for a Sabre with its wings swept at 45° rather than 35°, but the aircraft was radically different structurally and aerodynamically by the time it entered service in 1954. Enormous research had gone into the aeroplane and its systems, for the problems associated with supersonic flight were only slightly appreciated at the beginning of the 1950s. Carefully tailored lines, highly swept flying surfaces and enormous power were necessary to push the aircraft through the Mach 1 barrier to true

F-100 Super Sabres, though developed originally as supersonic interceptors, were widely modified in their service lives, and became potent fighter-bombers able to carry 6,000 lb (2,722 kg) of stores including missiles (Sidewinder air-to-air and Bullpup air-to-surface weapons), rocket pods, napalm and 'iron' bombs.

supersonic flight on the level rather than in a dive, and the power was found by the development of afterburners, which inject fuel into the exhaust section of an otherwise conventional turbojet to produce a thrust increase of some 50 per cent at the expense of horrendous fuel consumption. In the case of the F-100, the Pratt & Whitney J57-21A used in the F-100D model was rated at 11,700-lb (5,307-kg) thrust without after-burning, and 17,000-lb (7,711-kg) thrust with afterburning, to provide a maximum speed of 864 mph (1,390 km/h) at 35,000 ft (10,670 m). Another useful attribute of the turbojet was the considerably greater climb and ceiling it bestowed upon the fighter, the F-100D having an initial climb rate of 16,000 ft (4,875 m) per minute and a service ceiling of over 45,000 ft (13,715 m). This latter was relatively low by contemporary jet-engine standards. However, the cost of aircraft by the 1950s had confirmed the tendencies evident in the Second World War, that there was little need for aircraft dedicated to a mere single aspect of the fighter spectrum, and the Super Sabre was

Previous page: The diversity of weapons that could be carried by fighter-bombers of the 1950s is well shown by this Dassault Mystere IVA prototype: two 30-mm DEFA cannon, plus provision for an underfuselage pack of 55 unguided air-to-air rockets, 1,984 lb (900 kg) of bombs, two 19-tube air-to-surface rocket pods, and 12 T-10 air-to-surface unguided rockets, the selected combination being carried on four underwing hardpoints.

developed in several forms to suit it to different roles: the F-100A was the initial interceptor fighter; the F-100C was a capable fighter-bomber with inflight-refuelling capability for greater range, an underwing load of 6,000 lb (2,722 kg), and superior avionics for weapon delivery; the F-100D was a nuclear-capable fighter-bomber with maximum underwing stores capability of 7,500 lb (3,402 kg), an autopilot capable of guiding the aircraft at supersonic speeds, and other detail modifications; and the F-100F was a two-seat combat trainer, which had an inbuilt armament of only two 20-mm M39 cannon in place of the normal four such weapons.

The same basic evolutionary process that had produced the Super Sabre from the Sabre in the USA was used to develop the MiG-19 from the MiG-15/MiG-17 series: loje lines were cleaned up and elongated, much greater sweep angles were incorporated, and power was increased radically, though in this last respect the designers were forced to use a pair of relatively small axial-flow turbojets, the AM-9B rated at 5,732-lb (2,600-kg) thrust 'dry' and at 7,937-lb (3,600-kg) thrust with afterburning. Armament was finally standardised at three 30-mm cannon and, on interceptor models, four AA-1 'Alkali' air-to-air missiles that used beam-riding radar guidance. The mis-sile used by the F-100 was the AIM-9 Side-winder, infra-red-guided weapon of which two were carried.

Almost an exact contemporary of the Super Sabre, the MiG-19 has proved to be a more durable design, many hundreds remaining in service in the 1980s when most F-100s had been phased out. Where the

A powerful all-weather fighter, the Gloster Javelin was of the unusual tailed delta configuration, and carried the typical armament of two 30-mm cannon and four air-to-air guided missiles (de Havilland Firestreaks).

Far left: The Mikoyan-Gurevich MiG-19, code-named 'Farmer' by NATO, was the world's first production supersonic fighter together with the F-100 Super Sabre. A relatively uncomplicated aircraft that first flew in 1952, the MiG-19 was notable right from the start for its good all-round performance and considerable agility. This latter was rather discounted by US pilots, who saw in the guided missile the solution to all air-combat problems. Experience was to show them how wrong they were, and the MiG-19 remains a favoured and relatively effective air-combat fighter with many air forces in the 1980s. Illustrated is a MiG-19PM with four AA-1 'Alkali' air-to-air missiles.

Left: Such are the costs of developing modern combat aircraft that it is sensible to develop and adapt rather than design entirely anew, if this is at all possible. This tendency was well established even in the Second World War, and has been a feature of several important aircraft families in the poast-war era. The Dassault Super Mystere B2 illustrated is an example, for though it was the first European combat aircraft to have a speed capability in excess of Mach 1, it was a radical development of the Mystere IVA with more powerful engine, flying surfaces of greater sweepback and other detail refinements.

Below: The Dassault Mystère IVA was a French fighter-bomber of unremarkable but professional lines, and helped to provide the French air force with enhanced capabilities when introduced into service in 1955.

The capabilities of carrier-borne aircraft increased radically in the 1950s and 1960s, and jet fighters soon acquired supersonic performance. The first such aircraft was the US Navy's Vought Crusader. It is seen here, ready for catapult launch over the bows of an American carrier, in the form of the F8U-1E (later redesignated F-8B). This was the second production variant, which entered service in the late 1950s and brought with it a limited all-weather capability. Armament comprised four 20-mm cannon for close-range engagements, a fuselage pack of 32 air-to-air unguided rockets for salvo fire, and two AIM-9 Sidewinder missiles on the sides of the fuselage. The development of these missiles, the world's first effective air-to-air guided weapons, started the process of missile dependence that led to the erroneous elimination of gun armament in most American supersonic fighters designed for service in the 1960s.

MiG-19 has scored is in cheapness and basic simplicity, allied to the fact that it is still an excellent dog-fighting platform at a time when it is realised that outright performance is not the sole answer to all possible combat situations.

Other notable fighter aircraft of the same period, though not all had supersonic performance, were the French Dassault Mystère IVA fighter-bomber, the Yakovlev Yak-25 all-weather Russian fighter, the Gloster Javelin all-weather British fighter, the Douglas F4D Skyray delta-wing interceptor for the US Navy, the Convair F-102 Delta Dagger interceptor for the US Air Force, the McDonnell F-101 Voodoo multi-role fighter for the USAF, the Vought F8U Crusader fighter-bomber for the US Navy, and the French Dassault Super Mystère B2 fighter-bomber. All of these marked a considerable improvement over the previous generation of fighters not only in superior performance, but in better handling characteristics as designers came to appreciate more fully the requirements of speed round and above Mach 1, and advances in avionics, those increasingly important electronic systems that helped the pilot control his complex aircraft and weapons. And just as significantly, there was a gradual switch towards the air-to-air missile as the fighter's primary weapon. With powerful warheads, highly supersonic performance and inbuilt guidance, these seemed to offer a surer way of despatching hostile aircraft than the guns/cannon hitherto used. The air-to-air missile was being developed as an effective weapon during the 1950s in two basic forms, one relying on infra-red guidance to home on the hot exhaust of the opposition's engine, and the other using radar guidance (which came in several types) to home on the 'echo' produced by the opposition's metal airframe.

Above: By the late 1950s few countries could afford the luxury of one-role interceptors. One such was the USA, which developed the Convair F-102 Delta Dagger for just this role. Severe aerodynamic problems slowed the service entry of the type, which reached squadrons only in the middle of 1956 after a six-year development. The F-102, seen here in the form of a TF-102A two-seater trainer, was the first USAF aircraft to be designed for the carriage solely of missile armament (AIM-4 and AIM-26 guided missiles and 2-in(50.8-mm unguided rockets) launched with the aid of a radar/computer weapon-control system. *Left:* Designed as a long-range escort fighter for the Strategic Air Command, the McDonnell F-101 Voodoo finally entered service in 1957 as an interceptor and tactical fighter-bomber with Tactical Air Command of the USAAF. Performance and weapon versatility were keynotes of this nuclear-capable fighter's success. It was also developed as an effective reconnaissance platform.

THE MCDONNELL DOUGLAS F-4 PHANTOM II AND MIKOYAN-GUREVICH MiG-21

The emergence of the air-to-air missile, coupled with advances in electronics and aircraft performance, seemed to end an era in fighter design: what was now needed, the pundits decided, was a highly supersonic platform able to carry missiles to the point from which they could be launched to down a hostile aircraft as quickly as possible. Engine and airframe technology, the latter constrained for financial reasons to aluminium-alloy primary structures, meant that sustained speeds of little more than Mach 2.2 could be contemplated. This was nevertheless a considerable increase over the Mach 1.25–1.5 attained by the fighters of the first supersonic generation, and so a new type of fighter was born, marked in two different ways by the McDonnell F-4 Phantom II and the Mikoyan-Gurevich MiG-21.

The fighter that continues in service during the 1980s as the McDonnell Douglas F-4 Phantom II multi-role fighter began life in the mid-1950s as the McDonnell AH-1 carrier-borne attack fighter design. Before any hardware had emerged the US Navy altered the specification to that of a multi-missile fighter under the revised designation F4H for a two- rather than single-seat aircraft with improved radar and the ability to carry six missiles semi-recessed into the basic structure. What emerged as the F4H-1 in 1958 was a massive and angular aircraft grossing over 50,000 lb (22,680 kg), armed with four semi-recessed Sparrow medium-range air-to-air missiles and two more Sparrows or four short-range Sidewinder missiles on underwing pylons, and capable of a speed of Mach 2.4 (1,584 mph/2,549 km/h) at altitude on the power of a pair of 16,150-lb (7,326-kg) afterburning turbojets.

Right: The Phantom was the most important single aircraft of the US air forces in the 1960s and 1970s, and is here seen in the form of an F-4E with six bombs on two underwing racks, and with two droppable fuel tanks for long-range missions, which could also be extended by the use of inflight-refuelling.
Below: The Mikoyan-Gurevich MiG-21 may be considered the Russian counterpart to the F-4 in numbers if not in versatility, for the MiG-21 was designed as a light air-combat fighter.

Previous pages:
The most successful fighter designed in the West since the Second World War has been the great F-4 Phantom II, seen here under production at the McDonnell Douglas factory at St Louis, Missouri. The design began life as the AH-1 attack aircraft for the US Navy, but then became the F4H-1 carrier-borne fighter, and finally the F-4 Phantom II for service with the American forces. The Phantom entered service in 1960 and remained in production until the early 1980s. Upgrading of several variants of this multi-role aircraft is still in progress. Standard armament came to comprise of one 20-mm multi-barrel cannon, 10 air-to-air guided missiles (six AIM-7 Sparrow medium-range and four AIM-9 Sidewinder short-range weapons), and up to 16,000 lb (7,258 kg) of external stores carried under the fuselage and wings.

Early operations with the Phantom revealed that there was room for improvement in the accurate delivery of air-to-air and air-to-surface weapons, and better onboard computers were incorporated in the mid-1960s F-4D, though fuel capacity had to be reduced.

The Dassault Mirage III was the first European combat aircraft capable of Mach 2, and though designed primarily as an interceptor, was soon developed into a fighter-bomber and reconnaissance aircraft. A Mirage IIIE fighter-bomber is illustrated.

For its size and weight, the F4H was a relatively nimble aircraft that appealed to both the US Navy and the US Air Force, and under a service designation standardisation programme of 1962 the mighty Phantom II was designated F-4 after a brief spell as the USAF's F-110. In service the F-4 proved a remarkably versatile aircraft, usable in the air superiority role with its missile armament, and in the tactical ground-support role with underwing and under-fuselage loads of up to 16,000 lb (7,258 kg) of stores as diverse as bombs, rockets, air-to-surface missiles and chemical containers, supplemented as the course of the Phantom II's service career unfolded by other and yet more devastating loads. Despite its weight and size, the F-4B version of the US Navy had an initial climb rate of 28,000 ft (8,535 m) per minute, had a service ceiling in excess of 60,000 ft (18,290 m) and a combat radius of 500 miles (805 km), the

Lightning FI-A fighter refuels in mid-air from a Valiant tanker.

last extendable by the use of inflight refuelling. As combat operations in Vietnam unfolded, further models of the Phantom II were evolved for the US Air Force and US Navy, making the fighter (a word really incapable of describing adequately the Phantom II's capabilities) undoubtedly the most important of its kind in the world, and the most numerous Western combat aircraft since the end of the Second World War. And it is interesting to note that at the time of its introduction the F-4 was thought by many to be the ultimate example of its type: the missile had become apparently so decisive that future fighters would be missile carriers, designed to have high subsonic speed and prolonged loiter time so that this airborne missile and radar platform could fly economically at some distance from base, loosing off the occasional missile at hostile aircraft trying to penetrate the defended airspace.

The Russians opted for a more versatile defence force, with a mixture of fighters: the MiG-21 was a short-range dog-fighting interceptor, intended for clear-weather operations; the Sukhoi Su-9/11 was an all-weather interceptor; the Tupolev Tu-28 was a long-range all-weather interceptor; and the Yakovlev Yak-28 was an all-weather interceptor and attack fighter. These types were all in service by the early 1960s, just before the final outbreak of the Vietnam conflict, and provided the USSR with a wide variety of defence options in the air scenario. But the most important (in political, military and numerical terms) of these fighters was the MiG-21, a neat tailed delta weighing in at less than 20,000 lb (9,072 kg), less than two-fifths of the multi-capable F-4's gross weight. Powered by a 12,125-lb (5,500-kg) Tumansky R-37 (or R-11-300) afterburning turbojet, the early MiG-21s had a maximum speed of Mach 2 (1,320 mph/2,125

Above: Ever-inventive Lockheed went for a Mach 2 interceptor in the form of the razor-thin straight-wing F-104 Starfighter, which first flew in 1954.

km/h), a combat radius of only 100 miles (160 km), and a service ceiling greater than 65,610 ft (20,000 m). The Russians chose to maintain a gun armament, and the MiG-21 was armed with two 30-mm cannon as well as two IR-homing AA-2 'Atoll' air-to-air missiles. Range was clearly a problem, but this was improved in later models, and during the 1960s the MiG-21 was in every respect a formidable warplane, the best of its kind in the world.

Other nations evolved Mach 2 fighters, but none of them matched the MiG-21 or F-4 in military or economic significance. The UK had the English Electric Lightning interceptor, the Americans the Lockheed F-104 Starfighter and Convair F-106 Delta Dart interceptors, the Swedes the excellent Saab J35 Draken double-delta all-weather interceptor, and the French the classic Dassault Mirage III interceptor which was ready to enter service in the early 1960s.

Above: Careful assessment and courageous design allowed the Swedes to come up with the Saab 35 Draken, a high-performance double-delta able to operate from short stretches of road.

Below: The F-102 was never wholly satisfactory, so Convair redesigned the concept to fly the first F-106 Delta Dart in 1956. A notable feature of both designs was the use of an internal weapons bay to house the missile armament in an effort to keep down drag and so maximise climb rate in the intended interceptor role.

THE BOMBER AND ATTACK AIRCRAFT

Previous pages: The epitome of the heavy bomber in the Second World War may justly be regarded to be the Avro Lancaster. Evolved from the unsuccessful Manchester twin-engined bomber, the Lancaster was able to carry the heaviest bombload of any Second World War aircraft, and proved so successful right from the beginning of its career that only minor engine and equipment modifications distinguished the few marks to appear in a massive production programme.

BOMBERS ARE SPECIFICALLY offensive aircraft their function is to take the war to the enemy by unloading on him concentrations of explosive and other munitions, so affecting adversely his capacity to wage war. Within this broad specification there have been several types of bomber: the heavy bomber, intended primarily for strategic missions (bombing of the enemy's cities to break public morale, or bombing of key industrial/transport points to disrupt his military machine); the medium bomber, intended for interdiction missions in the enemy's rear areas, and for tactical support of the ground forces on the battlefield; and the light bomber, intended for tactical operations in support of the ground forces' mission. There are, of course, variations on this theme, but these three basic categories have generally been the norm. Though lacking the glamour of the fighters, the bombers are really the decisive arm of air warfare: thus the Supermarine Spitfire, a high-performance fighter, was tasked with

the problem of tackling the German fighters in the Battle of Britain, while the slightly less nimble Hawker Hurricanes went about the more important task of shooting down the German bombers which could inflict damage to airfields, ports, communications, factories and the like.

There was little to differentiate the bomber from the fighter in the First World War apart from size. Strategic bombing had been 'invented' but aircraft design, industrial capacity and weapon limitations prevented such a campaign from being launched as an effective war-winner; thus bombers were of the medium and light categories for the most part, 'heavies' such as the Handley Page 0/400 and V/1500 being relative rarities. Even the distinction between light and medium bomaers was little appreciated, but typical of the type was the de Havilland D.H.9A, powered by 400-hp (298-kW) Liberty inlines and capable of carrying a 660-lb (299-kg) load of bombs. By the standards of the day performance was lively, with a maxi-

The Farman F.50 was a French two-seat night bomber of 1918, and served in limited numbers until shortly after the First World War. Maximum bombload was eight 165-lb (75-kg) bombs, and the type's real importance is as a step towards the highly successful post-war Farman F.60 Goliath series, which appeared in bomber and airliner versions.

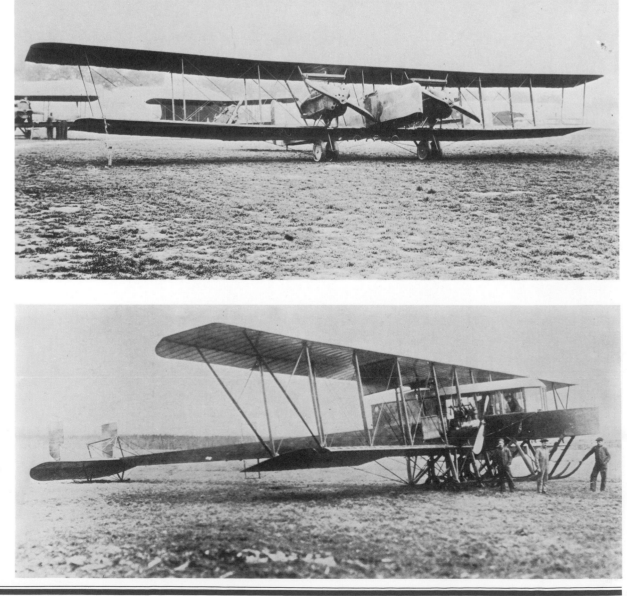

Though the Imperial Russian Air Service was lacking in distinction during the First World War, it was forward-looking enough to introduce the world's first four-engined bomber in 1914. This was the Sikorsky Ilya Mourometz, which could carry up to 1,124 lb (510 kg) of bombs over a radius of some 125 miles (200 km).

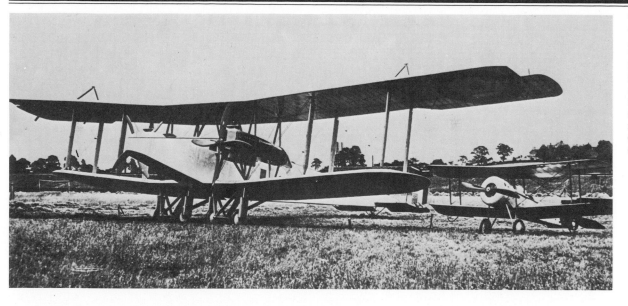

The Handley Page O/100 was produced in response to an Admiralty request for a 'bloody paralyzer' of a bomber, and entered service in 1916. One of the best aircraft of its time, the O/100 could carry 2,000 lb (907 kg) of bombs over a radius of some 350 miles (565 km), and had excellent defensive armament.

Early bombers were often marked by odd structural features in an effort to keep the flight equations balanced. Typical of this approach was the Gotha Ursinus G I of 1915, which had its fuselage attached to the upper wing of the four-bay biplane wing cellule, while the two engines and the somewhat flimsy landing gear were connected to the lower wing.

mum speed of 123 mph (198 km/h) at sea-level, and armament was the standard fixed machine-gun for the pilot and twin flexible machine-guns for the man in the rear cockpit. The heavy bomber differed mostly in size and weight, the Handley Page 0/400 spanning 100 ft 0 in (30.48 m) in comparison with the D.H.9A's 45 ft 11 in (14.00 m) and grossing 13,360 lb (6,060 kg) to the D.H.9A's 4,645 lb (2,107 kg). Power was provided by a pair of 360-hp (269-kW) Rolls-Royce Eagle VIII inlines, providing a maximum speed of 97½ mph (157 km/h) at sea-level. Armament was also increased, both offensively and defensively: up to 2,000 lb (907 kg) of bombs and a maximum of five flexible machine-guns. Larger bombers did exist (notably the German 'giants' and the Italian Capronis), but these were visionary rather than practical aircraft given the structural and power-plant technology of the day.

After the First World War much the same happened to the bomber as occurred to the fighter: limited development to keep abreast of advances, and initial reliance on the types that were best developed by the end of the war. Aspects of bomber technology that did receive some attention were important ancillaries such as bomb-sights, crew comfort, engine reliability and the like. And given that fighters should always have higher performance than bombers, and that because of their small size fighters are inherently cheaper, it is not surprising that air forces chose to further technological experimentation at this 'thin end' of the combat aircraft spectrum, with the sincere and not inappropriate belief that aerodynamic and structural successes won at the limits of performance could be applied also to slower but more expensive aircraft if the need arose.

By the late 1920s in-service bombers had not progressed far beyond the standards of 1918. The French Farman F 160, a four-seat night-bomber introduced in 1928, was powered by two 500-hp (373-kW) Farman radials, had a maximum speed of 109 mph (175 km/h), and could carry 2,205 lb (1,000 kg) of bombs over a range of 621 miles (1,000 km); the

Vickers Virginia was a comparable British type that entered service in 1924 and went through a protracted development history to produce the definitive Mk X, which was powered by two 580-hp (433-kW) Napier Lion V inlines for a speed of 108 mph (174 km/h), and had a maximum bombload of 3,208 lb (1,455 kg). Advances in the 'bomber art' were indicated by the provision of a tail position for the rear gunner, an auto-pilot and, in the Mk X, a primary structure of stell and dural, covered with aluminium, plywood and fabric.

Such biplane monsters could carry greater bombloads than their First World War predecessors, and were marginally better off for defensive armament, but had no real performance edge over the World War I types. The key to the bombers' success in any hypothetical conflict was thus that they could battle their way through swarms of defensive day fighters with their minimal armament, or alternatively avoid the issue entirely by undertaking their missions at night, when the fighters would be hamstrung by the additional problem of finding the bombers in this pre-radar age. Little thought was given by bomber protagonists to the immense difficulty of accurate navigation by night; instead, the works of prophetic doom by the protagonists of strategic air power were quoted as fact, and the public and services alike came to believe that 'the bomber will always get through', a tenet

Below: Typical of the financial impositions on aircraft design in the 1920s and 1930s, the Vickers Valentia was a transport (22 troops) evolved from the Victoria, but could also double-up as a second-line bomber, with racks under the wings to carry 2,200 lb (998 kg) of bombs. The type entered service in 1934.

Left: Designed to replace the D.H.4, the Airco D.H.9 was not in itself successful, as a result mainly of an inadequate engine. But it did pave the way for the great D.H.9A general-purpose two-seat bomber, which served the RAF faithfully up to the late 1920s.

Below: With the Martin B-10 series, which entered service with the US Army Air Corps in 1934, the bomber as a type entered a new era of cantilever monoplane construction, retractable landing gear and enclosed accommodation, this last including a turret for the front gunner.

Bottom left: The Douglas B-7 was an interim bomber type, with monoplane construction, retractable landing gear and metal construction (all relatively novel when the type appeared in 1932), but was let down by the fact that the wings were not cantilever units and so needed drag-producing struts.

that came to have stronger overtones during the 1930s and the build-up to the Second World War.

By the early 1930s it was clear that the biplane formula for heavy bombers was finished: the first modern monoplane airliners were entering service, and these proved beyond dispute that in combination with more powerful engines they could carry the payload of the biplane bombers over greater range at higher speeds, and thus more economically. Such monoplane bombers had been tried, on an experimental basis, with types such as the Beardmore-

built Rohrbach Inflexible for the RAF, but it was natural that the Americans, with their lead in the introduction of monoplane airliners, should lead the way with monoplane bombers. A number of experimental types appeared first (including the Boeing B-9 and the Douglas B-7), but it is to the Martin B-10 of 1934 that goes the distinction of being the US Army Air Corps' first all-metal low-wing cantilever monoplane. It was also the aircraft that effectively killed the biplane bomber among Western nations, and so led to the evolution of the definitive piston-engined monoplane bomber. However, it should be noted that in this respect the USSR was ahead of the 'free' world: as early as 1924 the Tupolev team of the Central Aero- and Hydro-dynamics Institute had started work on a low-wing bomber though this, unlike the Martin B-10, had a fixed landing gear arrangement. The Tupolev TB-1 was a metal low-wing monoplane, and set the pattern for a number of similar Russian bombers over the next 15 years. But whereas the TB-1 (bureau designation ANT-4) was in every respect an innovative design, successive bombers improved on performance by detail refinement and additional

power, but lost the technological edge of the TB-1, so that by the late 1930s Russian heavy bomber design was equivalent to that prevailing in Europe and the USA during the early 1930s.

Thanks to its advanced aerodynamic design, coupled with features such as retractable landing gear, internal bomb stowage and an enclosed nose gunner's turret (the first fitted on a US bomber), the B-10 was faster than contemporary American fighters, and thus proved an immense stimulus to the development of more capable fighters of monoplane configuration. But

Bottom centre: The Curtiss B-2 was one of the high points of biplane bomber design when introduced in 1929. The maximum bombload was 4,000 lb (1,814 kg), and a pair of gunners was located one in the rear of each engine nacelle. The example illustrated is flying under the control of a Sperry autopilot, one of the first such units and a notable advance of the period.

Bottom right: The Fairey Hendon, of which a mere 14 were built, was the RAF's first low-wing heavy bomber when it entered service in 1936. Essentially an interim type, the Hendon could carry only a paltry 1,660 lb (753 kg) of bombs on its two 600-hp (448-kW) Kestrel VI inlines.

the B-10 had in other respects only caught up with other military factors, for in armament it represented no real improvement: maximum bombload was a mere 2,260 lb (1,025 kg), and defensive guns only three 0.3-in (7.62-mm) machine-guns in three positions. The B-10 was generally superior to its European counterparts, principally in having a clean airframe without struts or bracing wires, and with a retractable landing gear arrangement. Monoplanes had appeared in Europe, but these were usually strutted, and the landing gear disposition generally favoured was the fixed tailwheel type, a measure of streamlining being achieved by fairings on the mainwheels. Typical of this European configuration were the French Bloch M.B.200 night-bomber, the Italian Caproni Ca 133 bomber/transport, the German Dornier Do 13 and Do 23 bombers, the Farman F 220 series of heavy night-bombers with a maximum bombload of 9,259 lb (4,200 kg), the slightly later

Above: The Caproni Ca 133 was a good example of the type of bomber/transport aircraft evolved by several European powers in the inter-war years for 'colonial' operations.

British Handley Page Harrow bomber/transport, the more advanced German Junkers Ju 52/3m transport/bomber, and the Italian Savoia-Marchetti S.M.81 Pipistrello. Though worthy aircraft, none of these matched the B-10 series in basic concept, indicating the widening gulf appearing between the Americans and the Europeans in the development of both medium and heavy bombers.

This gulf began to widen yet further with the development of two huge American aircraft to meet an official requirement for a very long-range bomber able to carry a substantial load. Not surprisingly, the two companies to produce hardware to the specification were Boeing and Douglas, specialists in the field of big aircraft to carry large loads over considerable ranges. The trouble with the two aircraft, the Boeing XB-15 and the Douglas XB-19, was that it was impossible to fulfil the specification with current engines: a new generation of engines, developing in the region of 2,000 hp (1,492-kW) was in the making, but until it arrived in the late 1930s, true strategic bombers such as the XB-15 and XB-19 could be little more than experimental machines of limited value except in the proving of advanced systems, the integrating of large crews, and the evaluation of solutions to the problems of long-range missions.

Below: Another dual-capable inter-war type was the Bristol Bombay of the late 1930s, which could carry 24 troops or 2,000 lb (907 kg) of bombs.

Top: During the 1930s the French aircraft industry produced some aircraft of virtually unequalled ugliness. The Farman F.220 series was a good example of this tendency. Speed was only 202 mph (325 km/h) but bombload was a useful 9,259 lb (4,200 kg). Seen here is an example of the F.222 with retractable landing gear.

THE BOEING B-17 FLYING FORTRESS

The increasing pace of technological advance in the 1930s meant that the Martin B-10 was soon obsolescent, and in early 1934 the USAAC issued a requirement for a more advanced multi-engined bomber. The requirement was more than met by the Douglas B-18, which was ordered in modest numbers, but well exceeded (in performance and also in cost) by the Boeing B-17, a much larger, four-engined monoplane with a number of advanced features. The B-17 Flying Fortress first flew in July 1935, and can truly be considered the starting point for the development of four-engined strategic bombers: it was a low-wing monoplane of metal stressed-skin construction, with retractable landing gear, aerodynamic features such as flaps, large crew, multi-gun defensive armament, and considerable development potential. More powerful engines were introduced during the B-17's career, armour and self-sealing fuel tanks were provided, and armament (both offensive and defensive) increased enormously. The definitive model of the B-17 may be considered the B-17G introduced in late 1943: this was powered by four 1,200-hp (895-kW) turbocharged Wright R-1820-97 radials, and could clip along at 287 mph (462 km/h) at 25,000 ft (7,620 m); service ceiling was 35,600 ft (10,850 m) and range with a 6,000-lb (2,722-kg) bombload was 2,000 miles (3,220 km); and while up to 17,600 lb (7,983 kg) of bombs could be carried over short ranges, the more usual long-range load was considerably smaller, total tonnage delivered to each target being made up by the hordes of B-17s that flew to them, providing the formation with good protection with the

Though preceded by some interesting experimental types, the Boeing B-17 Flying Fortress may be regarded as the world's first modern four-engined heavy bomber, designed principally for the safeguarding of the USA's extensive coastline but then widely built for the campaign of precision attacks on Germany's war-making industries and transport. Seen here is an example of the Fortress I, the version of the B-17C used by the RAF without much success as a result of faulty tactics and the type's unsuitability for operations in the technologically sophisticated European theatre.

Above: Later in the war, fully combat-worthy Flying Fortresses (B-17Fs are seen here) became the mainstay of the US 8th Air Force, which operated from bases in the UK to rip the industrial guts out of Germany while also cutting a huge swathe into her fighter and pilot pools in the process.

Below: The ultimate Flying Fortress mark was the B-17G with a nose turret to counter head-on attacks by German fighters. Here B-17Gs of the 381st Bomb Group head out on a mission with a P-51 Mustang escort.

Bottom: Shortages of transport aircraft in the Second World War often led to conversions from standard bomber models, as in the case of this Consolidated LB-30 Liberator converted to C-87 standard. This is the oldest Liberator still flying, in the hands of the Confederate Air Force in Texas.

interlocking fields of fire provided by each bomber's 13 0.5-in (12.7-mm) Browning machine-guns.

It was these B-17Gs that took the war deep into Germany from 1944 onwards, with the aid of escort fighters supplied by North American P-51 Mustangs. The Flying Fortress was the ultimate expression of the notion that 'the bomber will always get through', the type penetrating thick swarms of German fighters to destroy pinpointed industrial targets which included marshalling yards, canals, bridges, tunnels and port installations. In this work it was complemented by the excellent Consolidated B-24 Liberator, aerodynamically a more efficient

aircraft with better payload/range factors. The B-24 was the most extensively built US aircraft of the Second World War (no mean feat considering the type was a large four-engined machine), and found gainful employment in a wide diversity of roles, its most significant contribution being made as a maritime patrol bomber. Here the type's range and endurance allowed it to operate into the 'gaps' left by other Allied aircraft over the convoy routes, offering invaluable support in the decisive war against the U-boats. The B-24 proved itself a highly adaptable aircraft, with ever increasing armament, radar search equipment and a host of maritime equipment items in

its PB4Y-1 and PB4Y-2 forms.

On the other side of the Atlantic, the European nations soon to be embroiled in the Second World War had been developing their own improved bombers during the 1930s. The last fixed-gear monoplanes had been relegated to second-line duties by 1939 in most countries but Italy, and new generations of aircraft had come to the fore. Whereas the 1920s had been marked by such financial stringencies that most types had to have dual-capabilities (light bombing and army co-operation, for example) or were merely general-purpose machines (the typical Westland Wapiti was produced in various marks as a dual-control trainer, air-

Evolved from the Type 142 high-speed executive aircraft designed for Lord Rothermere, the Bristol Blenheim was the UK's first modern light bomber when it entered service in 1937. But service and public acclaim for the type's high performance obscured the fact that lightly protected and inadequately armed light bombers, which could do little damage even if unmolested, were in general obsolete as a type. Illustrated is a Blenheim IV.

control aircraft for service in Iraq, escort aircraft for service in India, overseas patrol aircraft, army co-operation aircraft, reconnaissance aircraft etc) the 1930s had seen the realisation that true excellence in the anticipated war between technologically advanced countries could be attained only by aircraft dedicated to a single role, or at the most two closely related roles. For the first time, therefore, there appeared aircraft that could truly be classified as light, medium and heavy bombers. In the light bomber category the British had the Fairey Battle and Bristol Blenheim; the French had the Bloch M.B.174/175 series, the Breguet Bre.691 series and the Potez 633 series; and the Italians the Caproni Ca.313 series. The Germans wisely ignored the light bomber type, rightly appreciating that its role was to a certain extent fallacious, an adequate light bomber role being possible with dedicated ground-attack aircraft, which would offer comparable support to the ground forces with a reduced chance of losses to ground fire.

In the medium bomber category the British fielded the Handley Page Hampden, the Vickers Wellesley and the Vickers Wellington; the French were more prolific with the excellent Amiot 354, the elderly Bloch M.B.200/210 series, the superior Bloch M.B.131, and the supremely elegant Lioré-et-Olivier LeO 451 series; the Germans relied on the trio comprising the Dornier Do 17, Heinkel He 111 and Junkers Ju 88; and the Italians used mainly the CANT

Left: Successor to the effective Savoia-Marchetti S.M.79, the S.M.84 torpedo-bomber adhered to the Italian penchant for the tri-motor configuration, but was not built in large numbers.

Right: As a result of its wings' great angle of incidence, the Armstrong Whitworth Whitley bomber always flew in a nose-down attitude. The type was one of the best aircraft fielded by RAF Bomber Command in 1939, and could deliver some 7,000 lb (3,175 kg) of bombs over a useful range. As it was phased out of Bomber Command it found gainful employment as a maritime reconnaissance aircraft and glider-tug.

Z.1007, the Fiat BR.20 and the Savoia-Marcetti S.M.79, all useful aircraft but troubled by inadequate defensive armament and limited development potential.

Heavy bombers were less popular in the European context: the Italians saw little utility in the type, the Germans had come to the same conclusion after the death of the type's chief protagonist in the middle of the decade, and of the other countries developing new aircraft, only the British and French had the economic and military far-sightedness to appreciate the capabilities of such aircraft. Several aircraft described as heavy bombers at the time were in service in 1939, and several considerably more powerful and versatile aircraft were under development as true heavy bombers. In-service types were the British Armstrong Whitworth Whitley, which in its Mk V form could carry a load of 7,000 lb (3,175 kg) and had a defensive armament of five rifle-calibre machine-guns (four of them in a powered tail turret); and the French contribution to this Allied force were the Farman F 222, with an offensive load of 9,240 lb (4,190 kg) and a defensive armament of a single rifle-calibre gun in three positions, the only slightly more modern Farman NC 223, with a load of 9,240 lb (4,200 kg) but the considerably enhanced defensive armament of two 20-mm cannon and one 7.5-mm (0.295-in) machine-gun, and the ancient Lioré-et-Olivier LeO 206, which though classified as a heavy bomber should more accurately be described as a medium bomber with its load of a mere 2,205 lb (1,000 kg) and three rifle-calibre guns for defence.

Below: The late 1930s were marked by a remarkable resurgence of design flair by French designers, who came up with such elegant creations as the Lioré-et-Olivier 451 medium bomber, which had first class performance and armament, but was available only in very small numbers by the time of France's defeat in June 1940. Some later served with overseas French air units and with the Allies when captured.

THE JUNKERS Ju 88 AND VICKERS WELLINGTON

Right: A unique German attack weapon of the Second World War was the *Mistel* (mistletoe) concept, in which an explosives-packed unpiloted bomber (here a Ju 88A-4) was controlled to its target by a pickaback aircraft (here a Bf 109G fighter). Once the bomber had been aligned to fly into the target, the fighter pilot released his own aircraft and escaped.

Above: The Junkers Ju 88 has a very good claim to the title of best bomber of the Second World War, and is generally accepted to have been the most versatile aircraft ever built. It was designed as a high-speed medium bomber, and is here seen in the form of the Ju 88S-1, which appeared in the mid-war years with two 1,700-hp (1,268-kW) BMW 801 radials in place of the earlier marks' Junkers Jumo 211 inlines to keep up performance.

Of all the bombers in service at the beginning of the Second World War in Europe, only the Junkers Ju 88 and Vickers Wellington proved to be truly effective types with potentials that were fully realised during the course of this traumatic conflict. The Ju 88 was conceived in 1935 as a high-speed medium bomber with limited dive-bombing capability, and entered service in 1939. It was designed as an immensely strong stressed-skin monoplane, with two wing-mounted engines, retractable landing gear and a compact fuselage able to accommodate a relatively small bombload internally. However, where the Ju 88 scored was in having almost unlimited potential for development in a wide diversity of respects: performance was constantly upgraded (or maintained with heavier loads) by the ability of the basic airframe to accept considerably more powerful engines, while the airframe itself proved admirably well suited to the carriage

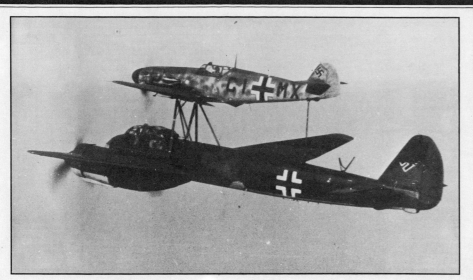

of remarkably diverse internal and external loads to exploit the full versatility of the design. The full catalogue of roles undertaken, with almost universal success, by the Ju 88 reads almost like a summary of the roles undertaken by all aircraft types in the Second World War: bombing, dive-bombing, torpedo-bombing, mine-laying, photographic reconnaissance, day-fighting, night-fighting, ground attack, operational training and even unpiloted bomb.

The Ju 88 maintained a 'radial-engined' appearance right through the war, for initial marks were powered by Junkers Jumo 211 inlines with annular radiators, while later marks had the BMW 801 radial.

The Ju 88 reached an early peak with the Ju 88A-4 medium bomber version of 1940: compared with earlier models this had a wing of increased span, a strengthened landing gear to cater for greater weights, and considerable improvements to both offensive and defensive armament. With a powerplant of two 1,340-hp (1,000-kW) Jumo 211J inlines, the Ju 88A-4 possessed a maximum speed of 280 mph (450 km/h) at 19,685 ft (6,000 m) and a range of 1,696 miles (2,730 km); bombload amounted to 7,935 lb (3,600 kg) carried internally and externally, while the crew of four (all located in a relatively vulnerable group right up in the nose) had two 13-mm (0.51-in) and two 7.92-mm (0.31-in) machine-guns to defend themselves. The A-series culminated with the Ju 88A-17, a specialised torpedo-bomber capable of delivering two 1,686-lb (765-kg) LT F5b torpedoes, (carried on underwing racks).

The Ju 88C series was developed as a heavy fighter derivative, and from this model evolved the Ju 88P anti-tank model. Various sub-models introduced different armament fits, alternatives including a 75-mm PaK 40 anti-tank gun, or two 37-mm BK 3,7 cannon, or one 50-mm BK 5 cannon, all formidable anti-tank armament, though the weight and drag of these installations degraded performance by a considerable margin. Further evolution led to the Ju 88D series of reconnaissance aircraft with a wide assortment of sub-types to accommodate different camera and equipment fits, and to the Ju 88H radar-equipped reconnaissance platform and Ju 88T long-range aircraft. The straight bomber version culminated in the Ju 88S series, which was optimised in the high-speed role with two 1,730-hp (1,291-kW) BMW 801G radials, providing in the Ju 88S-1 version a maximum speed of 379 mph (610 km/h) at 26,250 ft (8,000 m). Offensive load was reduced to 4,410 lb (2,000 kg), and the increasing difficulties in which Germany found herself later in the war was not reflected by any increase in defensive armament, which was actually reduced to a single 13-mm (0.51-in) machine-gun, the bomber relying on its speed and service ceiling of 37,730 ft (11,500 m) to avoid combat. It is difficult to convey the importance of the Ju 88 to Germany in the Second World War: what can be said, however, is that production of the type in all its forms totalled about 15,000 examples, and that the type served

The Ju 88 had only a small bomb bay, which helped to keep down overall size and weight, and thus to maximise performance. But many types and configurations of disposable weapon load could be carried externally, and here a Ju 88A-5 prepares to take-off with two underwing SC250 551-lb (250-kg) bombs.

with distinction from the beginning to the end of hostilities, and that it formed the basis of the much improved Ju 188 (about 1,100 built in a number of role-differentiated versions), Ju 288 unsuccessful medium bomber (only 21 built before programme cancellation resulting from powerplant problems) and Ju 388 reconnaissance bomber (77 built in the closing stages of the war). Perhaps the only comparable aircraft was the de Havilland Mosquito, and the comparison itself says much for the Ju 88.

The Vickers Wellington was an altogether more staid aircraft, but successful nonetheless. The key to the type's success was a relatively modern aerodynamic concept allied to the revolutionary geodetic structural method devised by Dr Barnes Wallis. This made the Wellington somewhat difficult to make, but resulted in an airframe of exceptional strength. The type first flew in 1936, and its immediate merits were recognised by substantial production orders within the British rearmament scheme. Early models were powered by the Bristol Pegasus radial (Pegasus XVIIIs, each of 1,000-hp/746-kW in the Wellington Mk IC), and possessed a maximum speed of 235 mph (378 km/h) at 15,500 ft (4,725 m). The offensive load amounted to 4,500 lb (2,041 kg) carried internally, and the Wellington Mk IC was judged to have sufficiently powerful a defensive armament to fight off German attack during daylight raids. However, early disasters did much to convince the British that this fit (nose and tail turrets each with two 0.303-in/7.7-mm machineguns, and two similar weapons in beam hatches) or even more powerful defensive armament would not suffice to allow the bomber to get through by daylight. So the British opted for nocturnal bomber operations, in which it was confidently believed that only minimal opposition would be met. But despite its failings in the day-bomber role, the Wellington still had an important part to play in proceedings, and further production centred on the Mk II with Merlin inlines, the Mk III with Bristol Hercules radials and the Mk IV with Pratt & Whitney Twin Wasp radials. All these were bomber marks, and production totalled 5,093 before a switch was made to a different role with the Wellington GR. Mk VIII, a torpedobomber and general reconnaissance variant for RAF Coastal Command. The change was prompted by realisation that the type's Bomber Command functions could more profitably be undertaken by the newer four-engined heavy bombers, while the Wellington's good handling, load-carrying charac-

teristics and endurance would prove useful for the 'poor relative', or Coastal Command. Radar could be carried, and armament could include depth charges or torpedoes. Further evolution led to improved maritime versions, and also to a substantial number of trainer and transport models.

However, the most prolific single model was the Wellington Mk X, which reverted to the bomber function, and of which 3,803 were built from 1943 onwards. This was perhaps the high point of 'conventional' medium bomber technology in the Second World War, representing the peak of the bomber concept inaugurated by the RAF in the First World War. Powerplant comprised a pair of 1,585-hp (1,182-kW) Hercules VI radials, sufficient to provide a maximum speed of 255 mph (410 km/h) at 14,500 ft (4,420 m), the normal range being 1,325 miles (2,132 km). Armament remained substantially unaltered: six 0.303-in (7.7-mm)

Browning guns provided a measure of defence, but increased power allowed bomb-load to creep up to 6,000 lb (2,722 kg). The Wellington, of which some 11,462 examples were built in all, is one of the unsung heroes of the war, for it went about its important work in an unglamorous way. But perhaps the type's most signal contribution to the Allied war effort was as a maritime reconnaissance aircraft, though the part in experimental work (largely in the development of powerplants and armament) played by the Wellington and its sturdy airframe came a close second. The Wellington was later in the war supplemented by the Warwick, a similar but larger aircraft powered by a pair of 1,850-hp (1,380-kW) Pratt & Whitney Double Wasp radials. Though the Warwick had been intended as a Wellington bomber successor, it finally emerged as an effective maritime reconnaissance and transport aircraft.

Above left: The Vickers Wellington twin-engined bomber served right through the Second World War, one of its chief advantages being its immensely strong airframe, resulting from the use of the geodetic type of structure invented by Dr Barnes Wallis.

Left: Vickers Wellington Is in flight. Much was hoped of the type in the opening phases of the Second World War, for a load of 4,500 lb (2,041 kg) could be carried over a range of 1,200 miles (1,930 km), and defensive armament of six machine-guns (two each in nose and tail turrets, and the remaining pair in beam positions) was thought sufficient to allow daylight operations against fighter opposition. But some severe losses in daylight raids to north Germany persuaded the RAF that only night operations could keep losses to an acceptable level, and so started the great nocturnal offensive against German cities and industrial areas.

THE NORTH AMERICAN B-25 MITCHELL AND MARTIN B-26 MARAUDER

During the Second World War the medium bomber came to be a weapon of significant import as its primary role switched from semi-strategic bombing, with quite large loads carried over moderately long ranges, to tactical support of the ground forces by interdiction in the rear areas. In this respect the Wellington may be considered the last of the old breed, and the Ju 88 the precursor of the new breed. In the newer aircraft great emphasis was placed on the reduction of size and structure weight: on the power of two 1,410-hp (1,052-kW) engines the Ju 88A-4 had to support a structure weighing in at 18,960 lb (8,600 kg) empty and spanning 65 ft 10½ in (20.0 m), while the Wellington IC with only slightly greater a bomb-load, had available only two 1,000-hp (746-kW) engines for an empty weight of 18,556 lb (8,417 kg) and a span of 86 ft 2 in (26.26 m). Such tendencies meant that the best possible performance was obtained from a

The North American B-25 Mitchell brought a new dimension to the concept of light bombing, for this powerfully armed aircraft (up to 14 0.5-in/12.7-mm machine-guns, sometimes a 75-mm cannon, rocket projectiles and 3,000 lb/ 1361 kg of bombs) combined its firepower with good performance to perform more like an attack bomber.

THE BOMBER AND ATTACK AIRCRAFT/143

Bottom: Japan's best bomber of the Second World War was the Mitsubishi G4M, code-named 'Betty' by the Allies. Though classified by the Japanese as a heavy bomber, to the Allies it was a medium bomber with a payload of only 2,205 lb (1,000 kg). Performance was good, but this was achieved only by omitting all types of protection and by making the structure light: as with Japanese fighters, the result was a useful offensive aircraft that could not take the punishment handed out by Allied fighters when the tide turned against Japan.

given horsepower, and that an increasing proportion of the bombload had to be carried externally on shackles or racks under the fuselage and inner wing panels. Such a method of bomb carriage had been used from the earliest days, but had hitherto been restricted mostly to light bomber types, epitomised by the great general-purpose Hawker Hart series of the 1930s. So far as the medium bomber was concerned, such a disposition conferred great tactical flexibility: small loads could be carried over longer ranges at high speed, or alternatively much greater loads could be delivered over shorter ranges at reduced speed. Moreover, the more compact but nevertheless stronger

fuselage meant that the nose was able to accommodate a wide variety of guns in the support role: these ranged between a battery of light/heavy machine-guns for attacks on infantry, light transport and soft-skinned fighting vehicles, to a 75-mm cannon (carried by German and American aircraft) for attacks on armoured fighting vehicles and shipping.

This tendency obscures slightly the distinction between the true medium bomber and the attack bomber. Perhaps falling into the former category were the Martin Maryland and Martin Baltimore among American aircraft, the Tupolev SB-2 and Tu-2 among Russian aircraft, and most of the

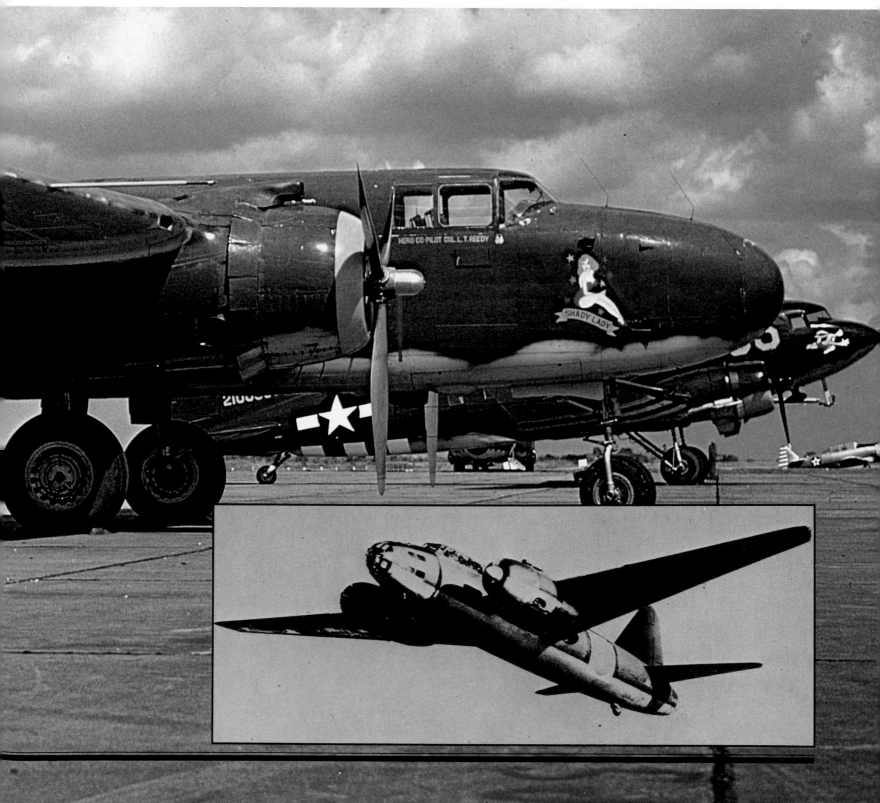

Japanese medium bombers (Kawasaki Ki-48, Mitsubishi G3M, Mitsubishi G4M, Mitsubishi Ki-21 and Nakajima Ki-49). The swing towards the attack bomber was visible in the Baltimore and Tu-2, however, and fully evident in the US Army Air Force's two classic medium bombers of the war, the North American B-25 Mitchell and the Martin B-26 Marauder. The most numerous of the early Mitchell models was the B-25D, of which 2,290 were built. This featured several improvements introduced successively on earlier models as a result of war experience: power was provided by a pair of 1,700-hp (1,268-kW) Wright R-2600 radials, and armament comprised a bombload of 3,000 lb (1,361 kg) carried internally and externally, and six 0.5-in (12.7-mm) machine-guns mounted two each in a fixed nose mounting and power-operated ventral and dorsal turrets. Maximum speed was a creditable 284 mph (457 km/h) at 15,000 ft (4,570 m), but experience soon showed that a much more potent weapon could be made of the Mitchell. The result was the redoubtable B-25H and B-25J series. Power remained unaltered, and as a result of greater weights (in part attributable to extra fuel for enhanced range) the maximum speed dropped to 275 mph (442 km/h) at 13,000 ft (3,960 m). But B-25H armament rose radically: maximum bombload was 3,200 lb (1,452 kg) or one 2,000-lb (907-kg) torpedo, and the gun armament comprised one 75-mm cannon in the fuselage nose, supplemented by four fixed 0.5-in (12.7-mm) machine-guns also in the nose, four forward-firing 0.5-in (12.7-mm) machine-guns in blisters on the fuselage sides, two 0.5-in (12.7-mm) guns in the dorsal and tail positions, and single 0.5-in (12.7-mm) guns in the two beam blisters. The B-25J was similarly armed apart from the nose installation: early examples reverted to the glazed bombardier nose of the B-25D, but later production introduced a solid nose fitted with eight 0.5-in (12.7-mm) machine-guns, providing together with the four blister guns on the fuselage sides and the twin guns of the dorsal turret a possible forward-firing total of 14 heavy machine-guns. The devastation that could be inflicted by this battery was awesome.

Like the Mitchell, the Martin B-26 Marauder was also an advanced medium bomber with tricycle landing gear but better performance, provided partially by the type's superb aerodynamic lines and the use of 2,000-hp (1,492-kW) Pratt & Whitney R-2800 radials. Wing area was slightly less than that of the Mitchell, despite a gross weight of 34,200 lb (15,513 kg) in the B-26B compared with 27,100 lb (12,293 kg) for the B-25A, and so low-speed handling characteristics were tricky, resulting in heavy attrition in training. But experience and a slight increase in wing area reduced this steadily, and the B-26 came to possess a combat loss rate to be envied by all. Successive improvements to the type's offensive capabilities resulted in the USAAF's definitive tactical support bomber of the Second World War, the B-26G which served in 1944 and 1945 with enormous distinction. Maximum bombload was 4,000 lb (1,814 kg), and 11 0.5-in (12.7-mm) Browning machine-guns were provided for offence and defence: two were located on each side of the forward fuselage in blisters, two were located in each of the powered dorsal and tail turrets, and three more flexible weapons were disposed to the nose and two beam positions. The importance of the gun armament and additional safety features such as improved armour protection, self-sealing fuel tanks and the like, is attested by the fact that bombload was actually reduced between the B-26B and B-26G models, the 5,200 lb (2,359 kg) of the early model dropping by some 1,200 lb (544 kg) to allow for the protective installations without too great a degradation of performance. The overall importance in the American armoury of the B-25 and B-26 can be gauged by the types' production, 9,816 and 4,708 respectively.

THE AVRO LANCASTER AND BOEING B-29 SUPERFORTRESS

Though several impressive heavy bombers were produced by the Allies and the Axis powers in the Second World War (the Handley Page Halifax, Heinkel He 177, Petlyakov Pe-8, Piaggio P.108 and Short Stirling, for example), it was the Avro Lancaster and Boeing B-29 Superfortress that deservedly emerged as the definitive heavy bombers evolved to meet the different requirements of British and American heavy bomber

philosophies. The British needed an aircraft able to carry a very heavy load over moderately long ranges at night, while the Americans were more concerned with a type able to deliver an equally heavy load with greater accuracy and from higher altitudes over very long ranges.

The Avro Lancaster developed as a successful adaptation of the Manchester bomber, a twin-engined design of admirable

The RAF's first four-engined heavy bomber of the Second World War was the Short Stirling, which was not very successful in its designed rolé. The RAF had ordained that it must not span more than 100 ft (30.5 m) so as to fit existing hangars, the resulting small wing area entailing a low service ceiling. Seen here is an example of the definitive Mk III heavy bomber version.

performance and capabilities beset by intractable powerplant problems with its twin Rolls-Royce Vulture inlines. With relatively little modification the Manchester was turned into the magnificent Lancaster by the substitution of four Merlins in a revised wing centre section. Of the crew of seven, three were gunners for the bomber's powered nose, dorsal and tail turrets. The two former were each fitted with twin guns, while the tail turret was a massive four-gun affair. The inexplicable fact remains, however, that the Lancaster like all other British bombers of the war remained underarmed, for the British stead-fastly refused to introduce the considerably more potent 0.5-in (12.7-mm) machine-gun, relying almost to the end of hostilities on the obsolescent 0.303-in (7.7-mm) calibre. Another fault of the Lancaster's defensive armament was the lack of ventral protection: such a position had been fitted to some early Lancasters, but was soon removed despite the fact that one of the German night-fighters' favourite tactics was to ease up into a position under the bomber's tail, where the British aircraft could be raked by the *schräge Musik* installation or merely by pulling up the nose of the fighter to use the even heavier nose-mounted armament.

The Handley Page Halifax heavy bomber lacked the glamour of the Lancaster, but was in many respects a finer aircraft. For apart from its nocturnal raids over the Third Reich, the type was also widely used for maritime reconnaissance, anti-submarine work, paratrooping, glider-towing and general transport duties. Seen here is a Halifax II Series 1 on a test flight just after being built.

Above: Italy's most powerful bomber of the Second World War was the Piaggio P.108, which entered service only in 1942. Despite a total of 6,000 hp (4,476 kW), which was about the same as the power available to the Lancaster, the P.108 could accommodate only 7,716 lb (3,500 kg) of bombs, and neither range nor speed were particularly impressive. An odd feature, well visible on this P.108B, was the three-deck nose, with the bomb-aimer at the bottom, the nose gunner in the middle and the flight crew at the top.

But despite these faults the Lancaster was a superb machine, to the extent that virtually no major development of the type proved necessary, the mark numbers being used mainly to differentiate between the different engines used: British Merlins on the Mk I, Bristol Hercules radials on the Mk II, and American-built Merlins on the Mk III. With four 1,640-hp (1,223-kW) Merlin 24 inlines, the Lancaster I possessed a maximum speed of 245 mph (394 km/h) at sea-level, a service ceiling of 22,000 ft (6,705 m) and a range of 2,530 miles (4,070 km). Though not very impressive, these figures indicate that the Lancaster had adequate performance. But where the type really scored was in its offensive armament: the bomb bay was a capacious affair, able to accommodate the ever-widening range of British conventional munitions without adaptation. And with slight modification the Lancaster could accept special stores such as the 'bouncing bombs' used for the 'Dams Raid', the 12,000-lb (5,443-kg) Tallboy and the 22,000-lb (9,979-kg) Grand Slam; this last was the heaviest bomb to see operational use in the Second World War. But the majority of Lancasters were used with conventional munitions, of which some 18,000 lb (8,165 kg) could be accommodated. Versatile and immensely strong, the Lancaster was produced to the extent of

Below: Russia, seeing little need for strategic air operations, produced only one heavy bomber type in the Second World War. This was the Petlyakov Pe-8, which had two unusual features in the provision of gun positions, each with a single 7.62-mm (0.3-in) machine-gun, in the lower part of each inboard engine nacelle, and the use of a fifth engine, located within the fuselage, to power the engine supercharging system.

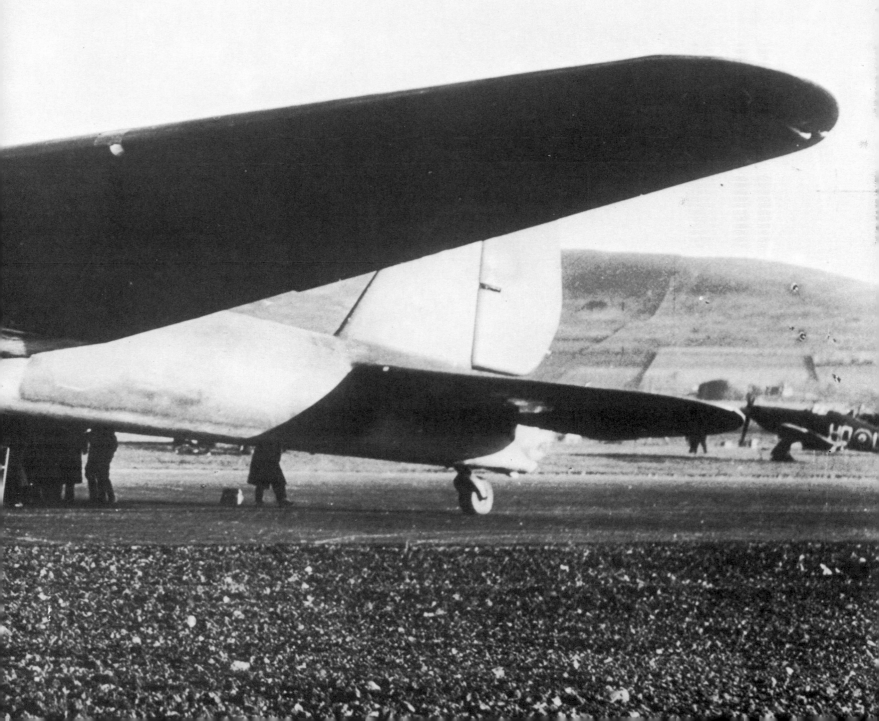

7,378 examples, and was the mainstay of RAF Bomber Command from 1942 to 1945. From it was evolved the more potent Avro Lincoln, which was just too late for service in the war, and the Avro Shackleton maritime reconnaissance aircraft.

The B-29 was conceived in different circumstances, as a heavy daylight bomber successor to the B-17, able to operate with greater loads over considerably greater ranges thanks to the provision of pressurised accommodation for the crew, and of a clean airframe powered by effectively turbocharged radials. The resulting B-29 was the synthesis of all Boeing's experience in bomber and long-range airliner design: spanning 141 ft 3 in (43.05 m) to the Lancaster's 102 ft 0 in (31.09 m), and weighing in at a maximum of 124,000 lb (56,245 kg) compared with the standard Lancaster's

67,000 lb (30,391 kg), the B-29 was powered by four 2,000-hp (1,492-kW) Wright R-3350 radials, the twin turbochargers on each engine allowing the B-29 to operate effectively up to 31,850 ft (9,710 m). Maximum speed was 358 mph (576 km/h) at 25,000 ft (7,620 m), and range amounted to a very impressive 5,600 miles (9,010 km), which permitted the Superfortress to operate against the Japanese home islands from bases in the Marianas islands, more than 1,600 miles (2,575 km) distant, with useful bombloads. As part of the B-29's totally advanced concept, a new type of armament was fitted, this comprising the standard twin 0.5-in (12.7-mm) Browning machine-guns installed in remotely controlled barbettes. Quite apart from producing the drag associated with conventional turrets, which could not have been fitted to a pressurised

aircraft such as the B-29, the barbettes offered the novel tactical advantage of permitting a form of centralised fire control, whose effectiveness was never fully tested as the Japanese could offer no real aerial opposition. The barbettes were disposed in forward and aft ventral and dorsal positions, and control was effected from blisters offering first-class fields of vision. The tail position was fitted with two 0.5-in (12.7-mm) guns and also a 20-mm cannon, and this was the only position retained when most B-29s were stripped of their armament to permit greater bombloads in the absence of fighter opposition. By one of the quirks of fortune that so often characterises warfare, the B-29 found its major employment in the night-bomber role so that it could operate at low-level with massive loads of incendiaries to burn the heart out of Japan's cities and

industries, high-altitude bombing accuracy having suffered because of wind speeds. Production of the B-29 amounted to 3,905, mostly in 1944 and 1945, and after the Second World War the type was developed into the essentially similar but more capable B-50 bomber while the US air forces moved towards a new generation of equipment.

Nor was it a coincidence that the aircraft chosen to inaugurate a new era in warfare was the most advanced bomber of World War II: on 6 August 1945 a B-29 dropped the world's first nuclear weapon on the Japanese city of Hiroshima, causing enormous casualties and damage; three days later another B-29 reinforced this ghastly lesson by dropping a second such weapon on the equally defenceless city of Nagasaki. The two occasions have since become notorious, even infamous, but there can be little doubt

The most significant bomber of the Second World War was the Boeing B-29 Superfortress, which ushered in the age of nuclear warfare with the atom-bomb raids on the two Japanese cities of Hiroshima and Nagasaki, but also burned the heart from Japan during 1945 with all-devouring incendiary raids. The example illustrated is on the 'strength' of the Confederate Air Force.

Above: Such was the range of the Convair B-36 strategic bomber series that it seemed like a good idea to give the type protection in the form of its own fighter, carried on a special trapeze under the fuselage and launched only with the advent of enemy fighters. Experiments, such as this combining a GRB-36F bomber with a Republic GRF-84F fighter, were only moderately successful as they called for exceptional piloting skills not available in most air force pilots.

Right: So large was the B-36 that the front and rear pressurised compartments had to be connected by an 80-ft (24.4-m) tunnel, through which crew members could pass on a wheeled cart. Efforts to boost the performance of the original piston-engined airframe (to meet the threat of the latest generation of jet fighters) took the form of two pairs of podded jet engines, one below each outer wing from the B-36D onwards. Maximum bombload, when nuclear weapons were not carried, was no less than 84,000 lb (38,102 kg), in the form of two 42,000-lb (19,051-kg) earthquake bombs.

that the destruction of these two cities and their people shortened Japan's end by months, thereby saving the lives of hundreds of thousands (perhaps millions) of military and civilian Japanese, as well as of substantial numbers of Allied troops.

With nuclear weapons the strategic bomber came of age: previous strategic bombing campaigns had relied on thousands of aircraft making many raids under all kinds of conditions, whereas the new weapon offered the possibility of comparable damage with minimum expenditure of resources and personnel. Moreover, the threat posed by such a weapon, it was argued, was the mightiest possible deterrent to war itself.

In the short term only the USA possessed the nuclear weapon, though this exclusive preserve was soon breached by British and Russian membership of the 'nuclear club'. For practical purposes, therefore, only these three nations can have considered seriously the build-up of a new generation of heavy strategic bombers based on the engine and aerodynamic research becoming available in the closing stages of the Second World War and immediately after the war's end. In the immediate post-war era only the USA could seriously contemplate the widespread introduction of new weapons, and she rapidly set about the development of new strategic platforms designed primarily for use against the juggernaut represented by Communist Russia.

The first such aircraft to appear was the huge Convair B-36, which had in reality started life in 1941 against an official requirement for a strategic bomber able to deliver a 10,000-lb (4,536-kg) bombload against a target 5,000 miles (8,047 km) distant, cruising at 35,000 ft (10,670 m) at a speed of some 300 mph (483 km/h) before returning home. As may well be imagined, the evolution of such an aircraft posed

enormous problems, and it was not until August 1946 that the first B-36 flew, some 15 months after the defeat of Germany, the foe against whom the weapon had been aimed. In one of the programmes most difficult to justify, the B-36 was pressed into service as a nuclear platform: powered by six 3,500-hp (2,611-kW) Pratt & Whitney R-4360 radials driving pusher propellers, the monster weighed in at 328,000 lb (148,780 kg) and spanned no less than 230 ft 0 in (70.10 m) in its B-36A initial production version. Maximum speed was 381 mph (613 km/h) at 34,500 ft (10,515 m), service ceiling of the

pressurised aircraft 42,500 ft (12,955 m) and range 8,175 miles (13,156 km). Thus the basic aircraft had to be considered in gigantic terms; so too did the armament, which could comprise up to 86,000 lb (39,010 kg) of free-fall nuclear or conventional bombs, and no fewer than 12 20-mm cannon located in six remotely controlled and retractable barbettes, plus a further two cannon in each of the manned nose and tail turrets.

Right from the beginning of its career it was obvious that this behemoth of the air was obsolescent. Odd measures were taken to try to improve performance, including the addition of podded jet engines under the wings, but even in the ultimate B-36J version speed was boosted only to 411 mph (661 km/h) at 36,400 ft (11,095 m) by the provision of six 3,800-hp (2,835-kW) R-4360-53 radials and four 5,200-lb (2,359-kg) thrust General Electric J47-19 turbojets. Maximum range of this model was 6,800 miles (10,943 km) with a 10,000-lb (4,536-kg) bombload. Other measures tried with the B-36 were the carriage of a protective fighter that could be launched and retrieved in flight, and the possibility of a nuclear powerplant!

THE BOEING B-47 STROTOJET AND BOEING B-52 STRATOFORTRESS

The B-36 programme represented a despairing effort to wring the last dregs of performance from an outmoded concept. By the time the bomber entered service in August 1947, the new breed was already in the final stages of hardware development. Not unnaturally, the first aircraft combined features of piston-engine technology and aerodynamics with the new powerplant to reduce the technical risks associated with the service introduction of the jet engine. Typical of the type was the straight-wing North American B-45 Tornado, powered by four jet engines and classified as a light attack bomber though able to deliver up to 22,000 lb (9,979 kg) of bombs. Similar Russian aircraft were the twin-engined Ilyushin Il-28 and Tupolev Tu-14.

The first definitive subsonic jet bombers were both products of the exceptional Boeing company: the B-47 Stratojet strategic medium bomber, and the B-52 Stratofortress strategic heavy bomber. The two bombers, which first flew in December 1947 and April 1952 respectively, had much in common despite their enormous differences in size: both were designed as high-wing monoplanes with their wings swept at 35°, their jet engines carried in pods set on pylons under the wings, slim fuselages and slender wings, and tandem-type landing gear (based on two bogies in the B-47 and on four bogies in the B-52) mounted under the fuselage.

Left: Characteristics of the Boeing B-52, the 'long rifle' of the Strategic Air Command, USAF, are a slender fuselage, massive tailplane, thin tapered wings and four pairs of podded engines. This is an example of the B-52H with turbofan engines, and visible are two of the B-52's primary weapons in the 1960s and early 1970s, the AGM-28 Hound Dog air-to-surface nuclear missiles.

Both aircraft entered service rapidly, and both underwent intensive development during the 1950s. In the final B-47E bomber version, the Stratojet was a powerful offensive platform, able to deliver 20,000 lb (9,072 kg) of nuclear or conventional bombs, relying on only a pair of radar-controlled 20-mm cannon in a tail barbette for defence, and capable of a speed of 606 mph (975 km/h) at 16,300 ft (7,395 m), a service ceiling of 40,500 ft (12,345 m) and a range of 4,000 miles (6,437 km). Power was provided by six 6,000-lb (2,722-kg) thrust General Electric J47-25 turbojets (in two pairs and two singletons), and range could be enhanced very usefully by the carriage of massive underwing drop tanks or inflight-refuelling from

the Boeing-developed aerial tankers that were a novelty in the late 1940s and early 1950s. At its peak the B-47 was employed by the Strategic Air Command to the tune of some 1,800 aircraft (in 1957), while many other examples were used for reconnaissance, weather research and other purposes.

The B-52 was of a different order of magnitude, and designed to provide the Strategic Air Command with its principal method of carrying devastating nuclear war to any point in Russia. Like the B-47 it incorporated a considerable number of electronic systems for navigation, defence and bombing, but posed for the Russians an almost insurmountable problem by its performance alone. (It is worth noting that Russia's

Above: The medium-range predecessor and partner of the B-52 was the Boeing B-47 Stratojet, whose lines and aggressive cockpit seemed to mark the type as a fighter rather than a bomber. This is a B-47A initial production example, all 10 of which were used for evaluation.
Right: The North American B-45 Tornado was the USA's first four-jet bomber, and was essentially a piston-engined concept turned into a jet-powered reality. Seen is an RB-45C photographic-reconnaissance version.

6065

contemporary strategic platform was the Tupolev Tu-4, an unlicensed copy of the B-29, of which several examples had force-landed in Siberia during 1944 and 1945.) Powered in its initial B-52B production form by eight Pratt & Whitney J57-19 or -29 turbojets in podded pairs, the Super-fortress turned the scales at some 400,000 lb (181,440 kg), and gave conclusive proof of its capabilities with two signal firsts: the initial air-drop of a thermonuclear weapon (H-bomb) in May 1956, and the flight non-stop circumnavigation of the world (with the aid of flight refuelling) in January 1957.

Successive improvements in operational equipment and engines marked the B-52C, B-52E and B-52F in the middle 1950s, and the next major improvement thus came with the B-52G, which had integral fuel tankage in the wings, raising capacity to 312,000 lb (141,523 kg) within the context of a 480,000-lb (217,728-kg) gross weight; the tail gunner removed to a position further forward along the fuselage, from which he controlled his weapons remotely; and provision for the carriage of two AGM-28 Hound Dog stand-off guided missiles on underwing pylons. This last was designed to allow the Stratofortress to loose off its weapons from outside the half-sphere of impossibly heavily defended airspace around major Russian targets, but still operate as an effective bomber. Bombs could still be accommodated in the bomb bay, as could special Quail missiles, small decoys designed to produce

The UK's initial jet bomber was the English Electric Canberra, designed as a radar bomber to operate at very high altitudes over long ranges. The type entered service in 1951, and remains in widespread use with the RAF and other air forces in the 1980s. The type illustrated is a Canberra T.17 trainer, used by No. 360 Squadron for electronic countermeasures training in the 1960s and early 1970s.

an image identical with that of a B-52 on Russian radar screens and so confuse the defences. Performance included an impressive maximum speed of 660 mph (1,062 km/h), a service ceiling of 55,000 ft (16,765 m) and a range of 10,000 miles (16,093 km), this last extendable by flight refuelling. For its time the B-52G was the ultimate strategic bomber, and the mainstay of the US Air Force's bomber force. But soon that service was to be faced with a tactical war of a type for which the B-52 had never been designed. It says much for the Boeing design team that the Stratofortress emerged as creditably as it did, and then went on to further improvement likely to keep the aircraft in service until the year 2000 perhaps.

As the other nations with truly strategic ambitions in the 1940s and 1950s, the UK and Russia also built jet-powered strategic bombers. The British felt the way with the classic English Electric Canberra, a highly manoeuvrable medium bomber designed to attack with the aid of radar, but in other respects tied conceptually to the piston-engined era. The type was produced in many forms and marks, and also produced under licence in the USA as the Martin B-57. Many remain in service during the 1980s. There followed a trio of so-called 'V-bombers', all intended to carry British nuclear weapons. First was the interim Vickers Valiant, with only a moderate angle of sweep; and then came two completely different but equally impressive designs, the Handley Page Victor, with a pod-and-boom fuselage, crescent-swept wings and a T-tail, and the Avro Vulcan, a menacing delta-winged design. All the V-bombers were powered by four turbojets, and the Victor and Vulcan could have proved useful aircraft if the British government had decided to place only one of them in widespread production. Events have shown the Vulcan to be the more versatile and long-lived type.

Russian heavy bomber developments followed two parallel courses: that centred round the turbojet resulted in the Myasishchev M-4, while that based on the turboprop led to the Tupolev Tu-20, a unique bomber powered by four immensely powerful turboprop engines driving contra-rotating propellers, and mounted on a relatively highly-swept wing.

The M-4 resulted from Stalin's insistence in 1949 that the Russian aircraft industry design a strategic jet bomber capable of attacking the USA. What appeared after an intensive design and construction period was the successor to the Tu-4. It first flew in 1953, and entered service in 1954 or 1955. The aircraft is a clean monoplane, with its four 19,180-lb (8,700-kg) thrust Mikulin AM-3D turbojets buried in the wing roots, and a landing gear arrangement similar to that of the B-47, with tandem main units under the fuselage and outrigger balancers under the wingtips. The original specification required a range in excess of 9,942 miles (16,000 km), but with a useful bomb-load of only 9,921 lb (4,500 kg) of conventional or nuclear weapons the M-4 could attain only 5,592 miles (9,000 km), and by the end of the 1950s the development of the type as a bomber was phased out in favour of a maritime reconnaissance variant, the 201-M. Defensive armament was made up of six 23-mm cannon, two each in forward dorsal, forward ventral and tail positions, the two former being remotely-controlled

Right: The third and last of the RAF's trio of V-bombers, the Handley Page Victor was like the Vulcan converted into a conventional bomber, and is here seen unloading 35 high-explosive bombs. Later use of the type has been in the inflight-refuelling role, and Victor tankers played a major role in the Falklands crisis of 1982.
Below: Russia's main strategic bomber of the 1950s was the Myasishchev M-4, potentially a powerful weapon system but ultimately one let down by range shortcomings. Subsequent deployment was in the maritime reconnaissance role.

Left: A great amongst greats, the Avro Vulcan nuclear bomber was the world's first large delta-winged combat aircraft when it entered service in 1957. Later modified to accept the Blue Steel stand-off missile, the Vulcan has undergone further adaptation in the light of tactical developments, being transformed from a high-altitude strategic weapon into a low-level conventional interdictor, and in this guise saw operational use in the Falklands crisis of 1982.

barbettes.

The Tu-20 (sometimes known as the Tu-95) appeared slightly later, and despite its odd appearance was an effective strategic bomber, and the fastest propeller-driven aircraft in the world. Its powerplant comprised four 12,000-shp (8,952-kW) Kuznetsov NK-12 turboprops, developed by German engineers abducted to Russia at the end of the Second World War, and the thrust developed by the four great 'contra-props' pushed the Tu-20 along at over 541 mph (870 km/h) at 41,010 ft (12,500 m). Range with a bombload of about 25,000 lb (11,340 km) was in the order of 7,767 miles (12,500 km). As in the case of the M-4, basic range could be extended by flight refuelling, though this was an art never practised as effectively by the Russians as by the Americans. The Tu-20 was developed extensively as a carrier of stand-off missiles, a type for which the Russians acquired an early fondness, and has survived into the 1980s as a maritime-reconnaissance platform of formidable range and electronic capability.

The only other nation to develop a strategic bomber by 1960 was France, whose Dassault Mirage IVA first flew in June 1959. In essence a scaled-up, twin-engined Mirage fighter so far as aerodynamics and powerplant are concerned, the Mirage IVA was designed as a supersonic medium-range platform to drop a single kiloton-range free-fall nuclear weapon. Powered by 14,991-lb (6,800-kg) thrust SNECMA Atar 9D or 9K turbojets, the Mirage IVA has an operational radius of about 1,000 miles (1,609 km) with a high-altitude cruise of Mach 1.7 and a dash capability of Mach 2.2 for crucial moments.

Right: The Vickers Valiant was the first of the RAF's nuclear-capable V-bombers, entering service in 1955. With this type were carried out the first air-drops of the British fission and fusion weapons (A-bombs and H-bombs respectively).

EARLY ATTACK AIRCRAFT

It may fairly be said that attack aircraft are descended from the 'trench fighters' of the First World War: aircraft such as the British Sopwith T.F.2 Salamander and German Junkers J I, designed to support the ground forces directly with machine-guns and light bombs, and provided with armour protection for the pilot, engine and fuel to improve the chances of survival at low-level and in face of concentrated fire from the ground.

But in the period immediately after World War I such dedicated aircraft disappeared from the armouries of the major powers: greater emphasis was placed on fighter and bomber aircraft, where the operators could

see a more impressive return for their money, leaving such money as was left for other purposes to go towards the purchase of multi-role aircraft. It should also be noted that the increasing number of independent and semi-independent air forces also had apparently sound military and emotional reasons for turning their attention away from the ground (support for the armies) towards the upper skies (pure fighter and bomber operations). The one major exception to this general tendency was the US Army Air Corps, which pressed slowly ahead with the design of two experimental attack aircraft (the GA-1 and GA-2, both built by Boeing), and procurement of small numbers of development types in the A (attack) category. The most important of these were the Curtiss A-3 series, evolved from the 0-1 Falcon and able to carry six

0.3-in (7.62-mm) machine-guns and 200 lb (91 kg) of bombs, and the Curtiss A-8 series, which evolved through a number of low-wing braced monoplane designs during the early 1930s, and had an offensive armament of four 0.3-in (7.62-mm) guns and 400 lb (181 kg) of bombs. The culmination of American experience with attack aircraft between the two world wars was the Northrop 8A, essentially a refined version of the Northrop 2 but fitted with a more powerful engine and retractable landing gear. Exports of the Model 8A went to seven countries, and small numbers were sold to the USAAC under the designation A-17A. Armament remained substantially unaltered from that of the Curtiss A-8 Shrike series, but performance was much improved, speed rising from 175 mph (282 km/h) in the A-12 Shrike to 220 mph (354 km/h) in the A-17A.

Left: Its experiences in the First World War convinced the US Army Air Corps of the 1920s and early 1930s of the value of attack aircraft for support of ground forces. Lack of funds prevented large-scale buying programmes, but the service tried to keep abreast of trends with machines such as the Curtiss A-12 Shrike, which had four forward-firing machine-guns and whose bombload could comprise four 100-lb (45-kg) or 10 30-lb (13.6-kg) or 10 25-lb (11.3-kg) or 10 17-lb (7.7-kg) bombs.
Below: Built by Boeing to a design of the Engineering Division, the GA-1 was an unsuccessful ground-attack triplane of horrendous flight characteristics.

THE JUNKERS Ju 87

Even before the A-17 (Model 2) and A-17A (Model 8) were fully in service, the lead in attack technology had crossed the Atlantic, where the newly revealed German air force was introducing advanced interim types while pressing ahead with the development of advanced aircraft. Thanks to the peculiar political organisation of the German armed forces under the Nazis, the Luftwaffe was dedicated in large part to the provision of tactical air support for the army, which was rightly considered to have the best potential for decisive influence in future wars. The medium bombers could provide interdiction of the enemy's rear areas, while the single-engined fighters provided short-range escort and interceptor capability, and the twin-engined heavy fighters would destroy any enemy bombers trying to interdict the German rear areas. But the ground forces

themselves, centred on the new armoured divisions which would strike swiftly and deeply into the enemy rear after punching a hole through the front line, would need the services of 'flying artillery' for close support once they had outrun their own slow artillery support. The result of this need was one of the decisive aircraft of the early war years, a machine still notorious as the 'Stuka', abbreviated from the German *Sturzkampfflugzeug*, or dive-bomber. The immediate stimulus for the Stuka was the Curtiss Helldiver biplane, which German officials had seen demonstrated with impressive results during dive-bombing experiments in the USA. The theory behind the concept was that a sturdy aircraft, its dive speed held steady by special airbrakes, could deliver one large bomb (or a few smaller weapons) with pinpoint accuracy by approaching almost vertically to drop its bomb at very low altitude before pulling out of the dive.

The first Ju 87 flew in 1935, and was succeeded by a number of revised prototypes as the company tried to iron out the

Stuka, the soubriquet of the Junkers Ju 87 dive-bomber, has become almost synonymous with the concept of ground attack. Seen here is an example of the definitive Ju 87B-1 version, which proved so decisive a weapon in the opening campaigns of Germany's expansion. A single large bomb could be carried on the underfuselage crutch, and four smaller weapons could be accommodated on underwing racks.

aircraft's structural and aerodynamic problems. What emerged as the initial definitive production model was the Ju 87B of 1938: this was an impressive aircraft, powered by a 1,200-hp (895-kW) Junkers Jumo 211D inline and capable of delivering a maximum bombload of 1,102 lb (500 kg) with total accuracy when flown by an experienced pilot. And the German Stuka pilots were experienced, having been blooded in the Spanish Civil War and then given all the training time they could use. Thus the first campaigns of the Second World War were marked by a string of German triumphs, spearheaded by the formidable Ju 87 opening the way for the German tanks. With its inverted gull wings, spatted landing gear, aggressive lines and 'Jericho trumpets' (sirens fitted to the main landing gear legs) the Ju 87 was militarily effective. But what few appreciated were the serious short-comings of the Ju 87 in its basic concept: the fact that as an aircraft it was slow and lacking in manoeuvrability, that as a combat aircraft it was woefully deficient in those aspects of protection that would allow it to survive against effective fighter opposition (missing from the first German campaigns), and that its success was attributable as much to morale factors as to purely military ones. In this last factor it should be noted that the Ju 87 was at first employed where the Germans had already secured the morale ascendant by invasion, so the defending troops were all the more susceptible to the terror imposed by the Ju 87's 'Jericho trumpets', pugnacious approach and alarmingly impressive visual head-on silhouette as it dived.

The myth of the Ju 87 was finally broken during the Battle of Britain, in which the RAF's single-seat fighters exacted a heavy tithe from the Stuka formations. The type remained a useful attack aircraft for another year, but only in combat situations in which the Luftwaffe fighter arm could ensure air superiority. Further development of the type followed, but little could be done to remedy the type's basic shortcomings, and from 1942 onwards the Ju 87 was increasingly relegated from dive-bombing to low-level ground attack with emphasis on vehicles and strongpoints.

The specialised armament required for this revised role further degraded the Ju 87's performance, and from 1944 onwards the type was a death-trap for all but the most capable pilots, a diminishing asset in Germany's air force. The main close support versions were the Ju 87D attack aircraft and its Ju 87G anti-tank derivative. Powered by the 1,400-hp (1,044-kW) Jumo 211J, the Ju 87D series was produced in several forms for day and night attack missions with bombloads of up to 3,968 lb (1,800 kg) and gun armament of up to two 20-mm cannon in the wings and a paltry pair of 7.92-mm (0.31-in) machine-guns for rearward defence. Even the fiction of dive-bombing disappeared with the removal of divebrakes during the variant's production run. The Ju 87G was an effective tank killer, if it could survive long enough to attack, for it was armed with a pair of 37-mm BK 3,7 cannon slung under both of wings.

But the performance of the Ju 87 was just not adequate for day missions, and from 1944 the dwindling number of aircraft available were relegated mostly to night missions as more capable day attack aircraft were evolved from high-performance combat types such as the Ju 88. However, one generally unsuccessful type pointed the way forward. This was the Henschel Hs 129, a conceptually advanced warplane hamstrung by powerplant deficiencies. Conceived exclusively as a 'tank-buster', the Hs 129 was a compact low-wing monoplane of great strength, with the forward fuselage as far aft as the pilot protected by an armour 'bath' proof against ground fire. The Hs 129A series was powered by a pair of 465-hp (347-kW) Argus As 410A inlines and had incredibly sluggish performance as a result of the low power and high weight. Matters were improved by re-engining with the 700-hp (522-kW) Gnome-Rhone 14M radial, but power was never adequate for the weight of the aircraft. However, armament was generally good: basic fit was two 20-mm MG 151/20 cannon and two 13-mm (0.51-in) MG 131 machine-guns, while additional firepower could be provided by a ventral pack for one 30-mm MK 101 or MK 103 cannon or, on some models, one 37-mm BK 3,7 gun or 75-mm BK 7,5 gun with the ballistic properties to defeat the thickened armour of later Russian tanks. The Hs 129 saw limited service in North Africa, but was mostly used on the Eastern Front, where the airframe's prodigious strength was not infrequently attested by the survival of the pilot in his armoured bath after a level crash landing at high speed.

Another ground-attack aircraft available to the Germans in small numbers, but which proved its utility despite its apparent obsolescence, was the Henschel Hs 123 biplane. This was an effective platform right into 1944, thanks largely to its considerable agility and strength, allowing it to avoid much ground fire and survive the rest.

The final approach of the Stuka to the target was made at high level. Once over the target area, the pilot of the Ju 87 half-rolled into a near-vertical dive and plummeted down, his speed held steady by the powerful airbrakes on the wings. The dive from about 14,765 ft (4,500 m) allowed the pilot to line up on the target with extreme accuracy, while the howl of the 'Jericho trumpets' crumbled the resolve of the defence. At about 3,280 ft (1,000 m), reached in about 30 seconds at a dive speed of 348 mph (560 km/h), the pilot pressed a button to initiate the automatic pull-out/bomb-release mechanism, necessary because he might black out during the high-g recovery from the dive. Thus while the elevator was automatically trimmed to pull the aircraft out of its dive, a timer operated the release mechanism for the bomb or bombs. When this had been completed, the pilot resumed control and climbed away from the target.

THE ILYUSHIN Il-2 AND PETLYAKOV Pe-2

With their preoccupation with the general superiority of ground forces, the Russians also developed an air arm dedicated to the tactical support of the army. Russian aircraft were generally designed to operate at only low and medium altitudes above the tanks, infantry and artillery below, and two quite outstanding aircraft were produced in vast numbers as 'flying artillery'. These were the Ilyushin Il-2 ground attack and anti-tank aircraft, of which some 36,150 examples were built, and the Petlyakov Pe-2 dive-bomber and ground-attack aircraft, whose production amounted to some 11,425 examples.

The Il-2, known to history as the *Shturmovik*, had already entered service with the Red Air Force at the time of the German invasion of Russia in June 1941, but only in small numbers and in its initial single-engined form, which proved not very effective. Like the Hs 129 the Il-2 was an immensely strong low-wing monoplane, also fitted with an armour bath that extended far enough to protect the single inline engine, fuel and pilot. As pilots became accustomed to their aircraft and learned to operate 'right on the deck', the Il-2 began to exact a heavy price for Germany's armoured advances, the armament of two 20-mm ShVAK cannon and two 7.62-mm (0.3-in) ShKAS machine-guns proving moderately effective, but the decisive weapon being the RS-82 56-lb (25-kg) rocket projectile, of which eight could be carried. Further capability was introduced with the up-engined Il-2M, with a 1,700-hp (1,268-kW) AM-38F replacing the 1,600-hp AM-38 of the Il-2, and the ShVAK cannon replaced by a pair of 23-mm VYa cannon with improved anti-armour capability thanks to higher projectile weight and greater muzzle velocity. But where the Il-2 and Il-2M were both vulnerable was to German fighters, and the design was recast slightly to permit the carriage of a second crew member, a rear gunner with a 12.7-mm

THE BOMBER AND ATTACK AIRCRAFT/169

Below: Operating at very low level, so that its cannon shells, bombs and rockets generally struck the target horizontally, the Ilyushin Il-2m3 was the greatest attack aircraft of the Second World War. A simple but effective design once the rear gunner had been added, the *Shtormovik* was produced in vast numbers, and posed a constant threat to German armour, transport, dumps and troop concentrations during the second half of the 'Great Patriotic War'.

Bottom: Though a larger aircraft, the Petlyakov Pe-2 was also an effective attack aircraft, and had much of the versatility of the Ju 88, combining performance with agility and varied weapon loads.

(0.5-in) UBT machine-gun, just behind the pilot. To cater for increased weights, this Il-2m3 was provided with a 1,770-hp (1,320-kW) AM-38F engine, and proved one of the decisive aircraft in history. Ever increasing numbers of the aircraft swarmed over German armour, infantry and artillery alike, causing enormous devastation with cannon, bombs and rockets. As thicker armour appeared on German tanks, the VYa cannon were replaced by 37-mm N-37 or P-37 cannon, and the disposable ordnance load of 1,321 lb (600 kg) could be made up of bombs (including up to 200 PTAB-1 or -5 anti-tank bomblets), or eight RS-82 rockets, or eight of the even more powerful RS-132 132-mm (5.2-in) rockets. Further development of the basic concept led, via the Il-8 prototype, to the Il-10 which entered service in the last four months of the war against Germany. The Il-10 was slightly smaller than the Il-2

series, but had better performance thanks to the provision of a 2,000-hp (1,492-kW) Mikulin AM-42 inline. Bombload was reduced, but the same types and numbers of rocket projectiles could be carried, and gun armament was standardised on two 23-mm NS-23 cannon and two 7.62-mm (0.3-in) machine-guns for the pilot, and a 20-mm cannon.

The Petlyakov Pe-2 was a larger aircraft, powered by a pair of 1,100-hp (821-kW) Klimov M-105 inlines in its early forms, and by a pair of 1,620-hp (1,209-kW) VK-107 inlines from the same bureau in its later developments. The aircraft was employed at first as a medium bomber or dive-bomber, but its performance soon commended it as a fighter-bomber and anti-tank aircraft, the bombload of 2,645 lb (1,200 kg) being supplemented or replaced by packs for 23-mm VYa cannon, 20-mm ShVAK cannon and, in the Pe-3 version, RS-82 or RS-132 rockets.

DOUGLAS A-20 HAVOC
AND DOUGLAS A-26 INVADER

Unlike the British, who evolved no combat aircraft specifically for ground-attack duties but relied instead on effective fighter-bombers such as the Hawker Typhoon and Hawker Tempest, the Americans' pre-war experience, and assessment of reports coming from Europe in 1939 and 1940, persuaded the US air force that the ground-attack aircraft had an important role to play. And while medium bombers and fighters were used with underwing bombs and rockets in such a role, the Americans produced more specialised aircraft, the Douglas A-20 Havoc and Douglas A-26 Invader.

The A-20 evolved from the DB-7 and Boston medium bombers, which the British had used effectively in the ground support role. Early models could more accurately be described as light or medium bombers with limited ground support capability, but with the A-20G the type gained a new punch with the replacement of the bombardier nose with a 'solid' unit accommodating either six 0.5-in (12.7-mm) machine-guns or four 20-mm cannon and two 0.5-in (12.7-mm) machine-guns. This provided an effective forward-firing punch in the attack role, and a target already softened up by the guns could be further hammered by a bombload doubled from the 2,000 lb (907 kg) of earlier models by the provision of underwing racks. Rear defence was also provided in the form of a new power-operated dorsal turret armed with a pair of 0.5-in (12.7-mm) guns, and the

Inset: In the hands of RAF and South African Air Force crews, the Douglas Boston II performed with great distinction in North Africa, and then moved across the Mediterranean to play as decisive a part in the protracted Italian campaign.
Below: The A-20G was a particularly potent version of the basic A-20/Boston/Havoc/DB-7 series, particularly when it was provided with a twin-gun dorsal turret (A-20G-20 and subsequent blocks). The example illustrated is part of the USAF collection at Dayton, Ohio.

type was given added tactical flexibility by provision of racks for a single torpedo, a capability much favoured by the Russians to whom most of the early A-20Gs were supplied. The A-20H was basically similar apart from having uprated engines which raised normal maximum speed from 317 mph (510 km/h) to 322 mph (518 km/h), both highly respectable speeds for a fairly large twin-engined machine.

Experience with the DB-7, from which evolved the Boston medium bomber, the A-20 attack bomber and the P-70 heavy fighter, made the Douglas design team ideally placed for response to a USAAC requirement for a new-generation attack aircraft, issued in 1940 and calling for a

Overleaf: Douglas A-26 Invader attack aircraft support the American drive into Germany during the winter of 1944–45 with bombs dropped round the outer defence zone of the 'Siegfried Line'. Clearly visible in this head-on shot are the Invader's fine lines and heavy forward-firing armament.

multi-role light bomber able to operate as an attack aircraft at low altitudes, and as a precision light bomber at medium altitudes, with performance parameters requiring high speed, agility and powerful defensive armament. Produced under the official designation A-26, the Invader was pushed through its development programme rapidly, and entered service in Europe during 1944, a remarkable feat despite the type's clear relationship to the A-20 since the orders for three prototypes (bomber, night-fighter and attack versions) had been placed only in July 1941. The third prototype was selected as the basis for a production order, though it was decided to forego the 75-mm nose-mounted gun that had featured in this model in favour of a nose installation of six 0.5-in (12.7-mm) machine-guns, defence being entrusted to remotely controlled pairs of 0.5-in (12.7-mm) guns in dorsal and ventral barbettes. But this was only the basis of the gun armament, which could be supplemented by eight more 0.5-in (12.7-mm) guns in four packs under the wings, and two further 0.5-in (12.7-mm) guns in side-mounted blisters on the fuselage nose, giving the devastating forward firepower of 18 0.5-in (12.7-mm) guns as the dorsal barbette could also be locked to fire forwards under the control of the pilot. Internal stowage was provided for 4,000 lb (1,814 kg) of bombs, while underwing hardpoints could carry a further 2,000 lb (907 kg) of bombs, or 16 5-in (12.7-cm) rockets, or eight rockets and two additional fuel tanks. The Invader thus provided the US forces with a new dimension of tactical air support purely from the armament point of view; at the same time the use of two 2,000-hp (1,492-kW) Pratt & Whitney R-2800 radials in an airframe slightly larger and heavier than that of the A-20 series, but somewhat cleaner aerodynamically, provided sparkling performance, including a maximum speed of 355 mph (571 km/h) at 15,000 ft (4,570 m) and a normal range of 1,800 miles (2,896 km). But despite the pace of the Invader's development and early production programmes, only relatively few aircraft saw combat in the Second World War, and large production contracts were curtailed after the end of hostilities. The A-26, which was redesignated B-26 with the termination of the USAF's A category in 1948, still had an important part to play in future American operations, as events during the Korean War showed. Moreover, the tactical versatility of the B-26 Invader immediately commended the type for further use when the US became embroiled in the Vietnam War in the early 1960s.

NAVAL ATTACK AIRCRAFT

The world's naval air arms, faced with the task principally of supporting their surface forces in wartime, were limited during the 1920s and early 1930s by financial problems, low numbers of relatively small carriers from which to operate, and the jealousy of compatriot air arms. This generally meant that carrier-borne aircraft of any category were usually inferior to their land-based equivalents during this period, not only for the reasons mentioned above, but also because they had the extra weight of naval equipment, such as arrester-gear, naval radio and the like.

But naval requirements also called for absolute precision in two sorts of attack aircraft, and in the design of torpedo-bombers and dive-bombers the naval air arms of Japan, the UK and the USA led the way. Navies had little need of conventional bombers, which were in any event too large and heavy for carrier-based operations, so the only way of delivering mortal blows to other ships was through great accuracy of delivery. Considerable strides were made during the 1930s, when the monoplane slowly replaced the biplane, though perhaps the most celebrated naval aircraft of all time, the Fairey Swordfish biplane torpedo-bomber for the Royal Navy, made its appearance during this time. An indication that naval types were beginning to catch up with their land-based counterparts came with such excellent fighters as the Mitsubishi A6M Zero and the Grumman F4F Wildcat, while an interim generation of monoplane attack aircraft (the Aichi D3A

A glorious anachronism in the Second World War, the Fairey Swordfish torpedo-bomber owed its survival to the skill of its crews and, oddly enough, to its dismal flight performance, with speed so low that enemy gunners found it hard to compute the right amount of deflection. The example illustrated is the Swordfish Mk II operated by the Fleet Air Arm's Vintage Flight from RNAS Yeovilton.

Far left: Despite its technical obsolescence, the Fairey Swordfish proved an admirable attack aircraft with a torpedo, bombs or rockets. Sporting 'D-Day stripes' are three examples of the Swordfish II, with strengthened lower wings to permit them to carry eight of the devastating 60-lb (27-kg) rocket projectiles.

Left: A Swordfish comes in to land on the carrier HMS *Emperor*, an escort carrier of the US Navy's 'Sangamon' class, often used for the support of assault landings.

Below: Armed with its torpedo, the Swordfish I was remarkably slow, but in some ways this was an advantage, for few anti-aircraft guns of the Second World War were designed to cope with such low speeds.

Right: With aircraft such as the Vought SB2U-1 Vindicator, the US Navy was able to evolve the dive-bombing tactics that stood it in good stead not only for anti-ship operations in the Second World War, but also for the support of US Army and US Marine Corps troops after the Pacific landings that took the Americans back across that ocean for the final defeat of Japan.

and Vought SB2U Vindicator dive-bombers, and the Nakajima B5N and Douglas TBD Devastator torpedo-bombers) was paving the way for more advanced attack aircraft taking better advantage of the possibilities offered by the latest engines combined with clean monoplane all-metal construction and retractable landing gear.

As in other respects, the Japanese failed to push on sufficiently with their second-generation monoplanes until after starting the campaign that dragged the USA into the war, and then it was too late to get adequate numbers of more advanced types into service before they were crushed by the USA's far superior economic strength, which allowed the nation to ride out the worst of the Japanese offensive and then fight remorse-

Below: So accurate and devastating was the bombing of aircraft such as the Curtiss SB2C-5 Helldiver in the closing stages of the Second World War that the torpedo-bombing function of machines such as the Grumman Avenger was little used.

lessly back in a protracted campaign for which the Japanese were not entirely or even prepared.

Thus the decisive carrier-borne attack aircraft of the Second World War were a trio of American designs, the Curtiss SB2C Helldiver dive-bomber, the Douglas SBD Dauntless dive-bomber and the Grumman TBF torpedo-bomber. The earliest of these was the Dauntless, which was conceived in 1939 as a replacement for the Curtiss SBC Helldiver biplane and the Vought Vindicator first-generation monoplane. The Dauntless was a compact low-wing monoplane centred round the two-man crew, provision for a 1,000-lb (454-kg) bombload carried on a crutch under the fuselage to swing it clear of the propeller before release, and a 1,000-hp (746-kW) Wright R-1820 Cyclone radial engine. The type entered service in 1941, and played an important part in the US Navy's first victories against the Japanese navy. Successive models featured uprated powerplants and improved armament fits (including the ability to carry depth charges or rocket projectiles), but it was clear by 1943 that the Dauntless was past its peak as a battle-worthy combat aircraft. Production continued into 1944, amounting to 5,936 in all, but from 1944 onwards the Dauntless was increasingly relegated to second-line duties such as anti-submarine patrol and training. The limiting factor in the design was essentially its small size, which meant that the obsolescent R-1820 radial had to be retained: in the definitive SBD-5 version only 1,200 hp (895 kW) was available from the R-1820-60, and this meant that although an offensive load of 1,600 lb (726 kg) could be carried under the fuselage and a further 650 lb (295 kg) under the wings, performance was

impossibly low at 245 mph (394 km/h) maximum speed.

The limitations of the SBC Helldiver had become clear early in the type's career, and a requirement for its replacement issued. The successful contender was the Curtiss SB2C Helldiver, a curvaceous low-wing monoplane employing the 1,700-hp (1,268-kW) Wright R-2600 Double Cyclone and sufficiently voluminous to feature an internal bomb bay. Early flight tests revealed problems as well as promise, but it was rapidly appreciated that the Helldiver had the potential to replace the power- and size-limited Dauntless. Development was protracted, and it was not until November 1943 that the Helldiver first saw action. Thereafter it assumed the main burden of US Navy bombing operations, proving itself an able weapon in the anti-shipping and ground support roles as the Americans moved back across the Pacific. Total production reached some 7,200 examples, and the SB2C-4 may be considered the optimum

Douglas SBD-2 Dauntless dive-bombers of Squadron VS-6, based aboard the carrier USS *Lexington*, patrol over the Pacific in October 1941, just before the USA's entry into the Second World War. The US Army also ordered the same basic type under the designation A-24, but then found that dive-bombing was not really suited to its operational requirements.

The Vought SB2U-1 Vindicator was a utility scout and dive-bomber. The first monoplane designed by the company, it was also one of the US Navy's first 'modern' monoplanes when it entered service in late 1937. The type had only a short front-line career, but was of considerable importance in the evolution of dive-bombing tactics.

The Yokosuka D4Y dive-bomber and reconnaissance aircraft, code-named 'Judy' by the Allies, entered service as a replacement for the Aichi D3A that had proved so devastating a weapon against Allied ships in 1941 and 1942. Like several other types of the Second World War, the D4Y Suisei (comet) was produced in both inline- and radial-engined forms, and was one of the best aircraft operated by the Japanese in the second half of the war.

version of this fine attack aircraft. This model was powered by a 1,900-hp (1,417-kW) R-2600-20 radial, which gave a speed of 270 mph (434 km/h) at sea-level. But where the Helldiver was most improved compared with the Dauntless was in its payload weight and versatility, in part a function of the later aircraft's greater size and power. The SB2C-4 had a gun armament of two fixed 20-mm cannon in the wings and two flexible 0.3-in (7.62-mm) guns for rear defence, but could also accommodate up to 1,000 lb (454 lb) of bombs internally and another 1,000 lb (454 kg) under the wings, though this latter load could be replaced by eight 5-in (12.7-cm) rocket projectiles for the ground-attack role. Further flexibility was bestowed on some models (SB2C-4E) by the underwing installation of a small search radar set.

The Grumman TBF Avenger was con-ceived as a replacement for the Douglas Devastator, but was fortunate to enter so widespread a service career: its chief rival, the Vought TBU, had superior performance, but as the design company lacked produc-tion space, the type was allocated for Con-solidated construction as the TBY Sea Wolf and was slow to enter service. Thus the field was left clear for the Avenger, which was in any event an excellent design with a mass of growth potential and considerable operational flexibility. Compared with its predecessor the Avenger was a much more massive aircraft, fitted with a powered turret for dorsal defence, internal stowage for its 1,920-lb (871-kg) torpedo, and the 1,700-hp (1,268-kW) Wright R-2600 Double Cyclone radial. Armament comprised two fixed 0.5-in (12.7-mm) machine-guns, one similar gun in the dorsal turret, and a flexible 0.3-in (7.62-mm) 'stinger' gun in an

Left: The Grumman TBF Avenger was the best torpedo-bomber of the Second World War, and was equally potent as a level anti-shipping bomber. A family resemblance to the Grumman naval fighters is fully evident.

Below: With wings folded, there is little to distinguish the Grumman TBF Avenger from the Grumman fighters apart from its larger size and deep fuselage, with a position for a ventral defensive machine-gun 'stinger'.

unusual ventral position that caught many unwary Japanese fighters; plus a torpedo or up to 1,600 lb (726 kg) of bombs in the bomb bay and, on later models, up to eight rocket projectiles under the wings. Few variants were evolved, so successful was the basic model, and production reached 9,839 examples. As with the Helldiver, some Avengers were fitted with search radar, and with the virtual elimination of ships (both merchant and military) as targets, the Avenger was gainfully employed as an attack aircraft in coastal areas.

The British, who were not faced with the considerable American problem of deploying maritime air power over vast expanses of ocean far removed from land bases, turned to the shore-based strike fighter as a better weapon, and several first-class designs emerged. The most notable of these were the Bristol Beaufort torpedo-bomber, the Bristol Beaufighter strike aircraft, and the de Havilland Mosquito FB.VI strike fighter. The Beaufort was a successive development of the Blenheim bomber, and served from 1939 to 1944 as a useful launch platform for the 1,605-lb (728-kg) torpedo, though this could be replaced by up to 2,000 lb (907 kg) of bombs or mines, making the Beaufort a weapon to be reckoned with in the European and Mediterranean theatres. But the Beaufort was limited by the lower power of its Bristol Taurus VI radials, which together provided only 2,260 hp (1,686 kW) to propel the 21,228-lb (9,629-kg) Beaufort I at a

stately 265 mph (426 km/h).

The Beaufort's strike role was ably taken over by the Bristol Beaufighter, a magnificent aircraft that reached its apogee with the TF.X model. This was a dedicated anti-shipping strike aircraft, fitted with centrimetric search radar in its 'thimble' nose, and given a maximum speed of 303 mph (488 km/h) at 13,000 ft (3,960 m) by its two 1,770-hp (1,320-kW) Bristol Hercules XVII radials. But if the performance of the Beaufighter TF.X could be considered marginally more than adequate, its armament can only be considered heavy and flexible: guns amounted to four fixed 20-mm cannon in the nose and one 0.303-in (7.7-mm) rear defence gun, and the offensive load could be made up of one 1,650-lb (748-kg) or 2,127-lb (965-kg) torpedo under the fuselage and two 250-lb (113-kg) bombs or eight 60-lb (27-kg) rockets under the wings. And if no underwing loads were contemplated, the forward-firing armament could be supplemented by six 0.303-in (7.7-mm) machine-guns in the outer wing panels. The Beaufighter TF.X was a devastating offensive weapon that caused fear wherever German shipping operated; equally fearsome, though available in smaller numbers, were Coastal Command Mosquitoes, of which the most powerfully armed was the Mk XVIII, which had a nose-mounted armament of four 0.303-in (7.7-mm) machine-guns and one 57-mm gun, and underwing loads of up to eight 60-lb (27-kg) rockets or two 500-lb (227-kg) bombs.

Above: Accurate information is the essential starting point for any realistic military operation, and during the Second World War photographic reconnsaissance came to assume a vitally important role. The best British long-range PR aircraft was the de Havilland Mosquito PR.34, developed from the pressurised Mosquito B.XVI bomber (illustrated). The Mosquito PR.34 entered service in early 1945, and had fuel in underwing tanks and bomb-bay tanks: powered by a pair of 1,710-hp (1,276-kW) Merlin 76s or 113s, the Mosquito PR.34 could touch 425 mph (684 km/h) and had a range of 3,500 miles (5,635 km). Cameras included two split F.52 vertical cameras forward of the bomb bay, and aft of it an F.24 oblique and two more vertical cameras.
Left: Undoubtedly the finest maritime strike fighter of the Second World War, the Bristol Beaufighter TF.X had centimetric radar in its thimble nose, a gun total of four 20-mm cannon in the nose and one 0.303-in (7.7-mm) machine-gun for the observer, plus a disposable load of one torpedo, or eight 60-lb (27-kg) rockets and two 250-lb (113-kg) bombs.

THE DOUGLAS AD SKYHAWK AND REPUBLIC F-105 THUNDERCHIEF

The tendency throughout the Second World War had been to reduce the basic size of attack aircraft, improving performance by increasing installed power and cutting down on structure weight. This left less space for internal weapon stowage, but offered greater tactical flexibility by removing the weapons to hardpoints under the fuselage and wings, which could accommodate bombs, rockets, fuel tanks and, later, gunpods and other advanced stores (napalm etc). The World War II experience was synthesised in the Douglas AD, which was too late to see service in that war, and was redesignated A-1 Skyraider in 1962. This was a true classic offering its operators unparalleled performance and weapon versatility in a relatively cheap single-seater. The core of the new Douglas design was the 2,500-hp

(1,865-kW) Wright R-3350 Cyclone 18, round which was schemed the smallest possible airframe, spanning only 50 ft 0 in (15.24 m) and weighing in at only 10,546 lb (4,784 kg) fully equipped in its AD-2 version. Inbuilt armament comprised a pair of 20-mm fixed cannon, but up to 8,000 lb (3,629 kg) of disposable ordnance could be carried on no fewer than 15 hardpoints beneath the fuselage and wings. The AD fully proved its worth in the Korean War, in which its payload, performance (especially long loiter time at low altitude), manoeuvrability and ruggedness combined to provide the US forces with the most capable attack aircraft of that war. The AD was apparently approaching obsolescence in the late 1950s, but new chapters were still to be written once the difficult tactical problems of air

Right: The Sud-Aviation SO.4050 Vautour entered service in 1956, and was produced in three versions for the French air force: the Vautour IIA single-seat tactical fighter, the Vautour IIB two-seat attack bomber and the Vautour IIN two-seat all-weather fighter. All versions had exceptional armament.
Below: Perhaps the acme of subsonic fighter development, the Hawker Hunter was transformed into a potent ground-attack platform when it became obsolescent as a fighter. Inbuilt gun armament was a quartet of 30-mm Aden cannon, and underwing hardpoints could carry bombs, rockets, fuel tanks and other disposable stores.

support in Vietnam were appreciated during the early 1960s.

The Douglas A3D (later A-3) Skywarrior was of an altogether more advanced concept than the AD, being based on the use of swept wings and turbojet power to provide the US Navy with a large strike aircraft with full nuclear capability. However, from Ed Heinemann at Douglas came yet another thoroughbred light attack aircraft, the A4D (later A-4) Skyhawk. Heinemann's logical, but almost universally disbelieved, design philosophy was that attack aircraft were becoming too heavy, too complex and too expensive to make them truly effective. He therefore set about producing an attack aircraft of the lowest possible structure weight, systems as simple as was compatible with the intended role, and large external payload in the fashion of the AD. The result was a small tailed delta-wing aircraft with stalky landing gear to permit the carriage of external stores on three hardpoints. Produc-

tion examples of the Skyhawk began to enter service in 1956, and US Navy pilots immediately found themselves in an aircraft with superb handling, spritely performance and heavyweight punch: armament consisted of two inbuilt 20-mm cannon and up to 5,000 lb (2,268 kg) of rockets, bombs, gun pods, fuel tanks and even a new weapon, the Bullpup air-to-surface guided missile.

The fighter-bomber reached an impressive peak with the Republic F-105 Thunderchief, a nuclear-capable tactical aircraft which first flew in 1955. The massive weapons bay in the fuselage can accommodate up to 8,000 lb (3,629 kg) of stores. High supersonic performance (Mach 2+) was always envisaged.

Further improvements followed, and by 1960 Heinemann was working on the A4D-5 (A-4E) with the 8,500-lb (3,856-kg) thrust Pratt & Whitney J52-6A engine in place of the earlier models' Wright J65, a licence-built version of the British Armstrong Siddeley Sapphire turbojet. This engine was less fuel-thirsty than the J65, resulting in an increase in unrefuelled range. The airframe was re-engineered, and disposable load rose to 8,200 lb (3,720 kg) carried on one underfuselage and four underwing hard-points.

This A4D-5 Skyhawk was truly a great attack aircraft, offering performance, flexibility and the ability to get right down with the troops on the ground. The USAF, how-ever, was wedded to the concept of nuclear strike at supersonic speeds, and it intro-duced to service in 1959 the massive Repub-lic F-105 Thunderchief. This was powered

by an afterburning Pratt & Whitney J75 turbojet, weighed in at a maximum of some 52,000 lb (23,587 kg) compared with the A4D-5's 24,500 lb (11,113 kg), but was cap-able of about Mach 2 at high altitude. Intended principally for the interdiction role in Europe, the Thunderchief's primary weapon was the free-fall nuclear bomb, of which some 8,000 lb (3,628 kg) could be carried internally. Greater flexibility was offered if a conventional load was carried, for the internal stowage could then be boosted by a further 4,000 lb (1,814 kg) carried under the fuselage and wings. As with the A4D, early examples of American air-to-surface missiles could also be fitted.

The US Navy and US Air Force thus went in for radically different approaches to the concept of attack aircraft, the former opting for a lightweight platform offering great flexibility in the tactical role, and the

latter for a supersonic heavyweight optimised for the anticipated decisive battle in Europe against the Russians. But what the US Air Force had failed to take into account was that it might become tangled into a small-scale war where supersonic, complex aircraft were not only unnecessary but actually an embarrassment. The Vietnam War was going to change a lot of military aviation thinking, resulting in a totally new generation of aircraft. And this rethinking was to apply, moreover, not just to attack aircraft, but also to fighters and bombers in all their various forms. Experience and technological advance since the Second World War had convinced many, notably the Americans, that performance was all. Vietnam was to show them that the age-old virtues of easy maintenance, manoeuvrability and tactical versatility were still prerequisites of a successful warplane. Per-

formance was still needed, but it could not be won to the detriment of other factors. To a certain extent the Russians and other European powers were more fortunate in this respect, for their sights were more firmly fixed on local problems, where the USAF's concept was still valid.

As it was, however, the Europeans and Russians were slightly behind the Americans in the introduction of new attack aircraft, and European reliance was still based on elderly American types, ground-attack versions of the Hawker Hunter, the Dassault Super Mystere B2 and the SNCASO SO 4050 Vautour. Later aircraft were in the gestatory period, and the Russians had recently adopted the Sukhoi Su-7 attack aircraft, but the amount of rethinking necessary as a result of the Vietnam War and other conflicts of the 1960s was to be considerably less.

The F-105D's capabilities were much enhanced by addition of a General Electric FC-5 integrated fire-control and automatic flight system, which included an autopilot, a Doppler navigator, an air-data computer, search and range radar, missile-launch computer and a toss-bomb computer. The effect of these modifications was to ensure the accurate delivery of more than 14,000 lb (6,350 kg) of internal and external stores. Production began in 1960.

GENERAL INDEX

Aerodynamics, 43, 125, 128, 140, 145, 152, 154, 161, 167, 173
Automatic flight control, 93
Avionics, 102, 109

Battle of Britain, 32, 45–6, 120, 167
Beisel, Tex, 73
Bell, Larry, 52
Blitz (1940–41), 76
Bombs: 'bouncing', 149; Grand Slam, 149; PTAB-1, 169; Tallboy, 149
'Bubble' canopy, 51

Cannon: Aden, 93; BK 3, 7, 138, 167; BK 5, 138; Hispano, 46, 51, 77; M 39, 102; MG FF, 37; MG 151, 20, 79, 167; Mk 101, 167; Mk 103, 167; N-37, 169; NS-11-P-37, 68; NS-23, 169; NS-P-45, 68; P-37, 169; ShVAK, 66–7, 168–69; VYa, 168–69; VYa-23V, 68

Engines:
  AM-9B turbojet, 103; AM-35A inline, 65; AM-38, 168; AM-38F, 168–69
  ABC Dragonfly radial, 13
  Allison, 35; V-1710 inline, 53, 56–7, 62, 69
  Argus As410A inline, 167
  Armstrong Siddeley: Jaguar radial, 13; Sapphire turbojet, 188
  Bristol: Centarurus radial piston, 51; Hercules radial, 140, 149, 185; Pegasus radial, 140; Taurus VI radial, 185
  BMW 801 radial, 78–9, 137; 801G radial, 139
  Carburetted, 37
  Curtiss V-1570-23 Conqueror 'C' inline, 13
  Daimler-Benz: DB600, 34; DB601, 43, 53; DB603, 78; DB605A, 40, 53; DB605D, 37, 53; DB 605L, 37, 53
  Farman radial, 121
  Fuel-injected, 37
  Gas-turbine, 82
  General Electric: J47-19 turbojet, 153; J47-25 turbojet, 156; J-47-37 turbojet, 92; J73, 93
  Gnome-Rhone 14M radial, 167
  Hispano-Suiza 12Y, 35, 66
  Jaguar LV, 13
  Jet, 82, 85, 88, 154, 156–60
  Junkers: Jumo 210, 34–5; Jumo 211 inline, 137; Jumo 211D inline, 167; Jumo 211J inline, 138, 167; Jumo 213 inline, 40, 79
  Klimov: M-105 inline, 169; M-105P, 66; M-105PF, 66; M-107, 67; VK-105PF-2, 67
  Kuznetsov NK-12 turboprop, 161
  Liberty inline, 120
  Merlin (American) inline, 149
  Mikulin: AM-3D turbojet, 160; AM-35 inline, 65; AM-42 inline, 169
  Napier: Lion V inline, 122; Sabre, 11, 49; Sabre 11B/Sabre VA inline piston, 51
  Piston, 69, 82, 124, 154
  Pratt & Whitney: Double Wasp radial, 141; J-52-6A, 188; J-57-19 turbojet, 188; R-1340 Wasp, 16, 53; R-1830 Twin Wasp, 33, 140; R-2600-20 radial, 181; R-2800 radial, 61, 145, 173; R-2800 22W Double Wasp radial, 61, 64, 73–4; R-2800-10 Double Wasp,

81; R-4360 radial, 152–53
RD-45FA, 92; RD-45/VK-1, 92
Radial, 12, 13, 15, 28, 34, 40, 61
Renault, 9
Rolls Royce: Avon R.A.7 turbojet, 93; Eagle VIII inline, 121; Griffon, 48–9, 53; Kestrel, 35; Merlin, 44–6, 48, 53, 57, 76–7, 140, 147, 149; Merlin-V-1650-3, 69; Nene, 92; Vulture inline, 147
Rotary piston, 9
Shvetsov ASh-82 radial, 66–7; ASh-82A, 66; ASh-82FN, 66; ASh FNV, 66; M-62 radial, 28
SNECMA: Atar 92 turbojet, 161; Atar 9K turbojet, 161
Supercharged, 9, 40, 66
Tumansky R-37 turbojet, 116
Turbocharger, 62, 64; General Electric exhaust-driven, 62, 150
Turbojet, 99, 112, 160, 187
Turboprop, 160
VK-1A, 92; VK-105PF, 67–8; VK-105PF-1, 68; VK-105PF-3, 68; VK-105RD, 68; VK-107 inline, 169; VK-107A, 67–8
Wright, 53; J65, 188; R-1820 Cyclone radial, 180; R-1820-60, 180; R-1820-78 Cyclone 9 radial, 16, 33; R-1820-97 radial, 128; R-2600 Cyclone 14, 66–7, 144; R-2600 Double Cyclone, 180–81; R-3350 Cyclone 18, 186; R-3350 radial, 150

'Galland' hood, 37
Gorbunov, Vladimir, 65
Gudkov, Mikhsil, 65
Guns: Pak 40 anti-tank, 138; 'stinger', 181
Gurevich, Mikhail, 65

Heinemann, Ed, 187–88
Hendon RAF Display (1930), 131
Hiroshima, 150

Imperial Japanese Army, 25, 42
Imperial Japanese Navy, 25, 42, 180
Italo-Turkish War (1911–12), 8

Kartveli, Alexander, 62
Korean War, 75, 88, 92, 173, 186

Landing-gear: fixed, 42, 126, 131; narrow-track, 44; retractable, 17, 28, 42, 125–26, 128, 136, 163, 179; stalky, 187; tandem-type, 156; tricycle, 57, 145
Lavochkin, Semyon, 65
Luftwaffe, 32, 76–7, 165, 167

Mach 1, 98, 109; Mach 1.7, 161; Mach 2, 116–17, 188; Mach 2.2, 112, 161; Mach 2.4, 112
Machine guns: BK 3, 7, 167; BK 7, 5, 167; Beresin UB, 67–8; Browning, 46, 64, 74, 130, 141, 145; MG 17, 37; MG 131, 37, 167; ShKAS, 67, 168; UBT, 169
Messerschmitt, Willi, 34
Mikoyan, Artem, 65
Missiles, 93, 103, 109, 187–88; AA-1 'Alkali', 103, 104; AA-2 'Atoll', 117; AHM-28 Hound Dog, 158; AIM-9 Sidewinder, 93, 103, 112; Bullpup, 187; Quail, 159; Sparrow, 112; Stand-off, 161
Mitchell, Reginald, 44
Monocoque, 21

Nagasaki, 150
Nomonhan Incident, 29
North African theatre, 44
North Atlantic Treaty Organisation

(NATO), 93
Nuclear warfare, 152–53, 156–57, 159–61, 187–88

Pacific Theatre, 62, 74
Polikarpov, Nikolai, 25

Radar, 46, 76–9, 93, 96, 103, 109, 130, 140, 156, 159, 185; Airborne Interception Mk IV, 77; Centimetric search, 185; FuG 218 Neptun VR, 79; FuG 220 Lichtenstein SM-2, 79; FuG 228 Lichtenstein SN-3, 79; SCR-720 (A1 Mk 10), 77
Rockets: Folding-Fin aircraft, 93; RS-82, 168–69; RS-132, 169
Royal Air Force, 13, 44, 46, 62, 69, 97, 140, 167; Bomber Command, 140, 150; Coastal Command, 140, 185; Fighter Command, 46

Schneider Trophy, 35
Sesquiplane, 13, 15
Soviet Air Force, 168
Spanish Civil War, 167
Supersonic flight, 98–9, 102, 109, 188–89

Tank, Kurt, 40
Tupolev, Andrei, 25

US Air Force, 37, 62, 93, 96, 109, 114–15, 173, 188–89; Strategic Air Command, 156
US Army, 15–16; Air Corps, 22, 124, 128, 163, 171; Air Force, 37, 52, 56, 61–2, 69, 144–45, 170
US Navy, 15, 16, 17, 52, 61, 73, 93, 96, 109, 112, 114–15, 180, 187–88; Fleet Air Arm, 73

Vietnamese War, 115–16, 173, 187, 189

Wallis, Dr Barnes, 140
Wing types: Delta, 109, 116–17, 160, 187; High, 24; Low, 24, 28, 125, 163, 168, 180; Parasol, 22, 24; Swept, 85, 93, 96, 98, 154, 159, 187
World War I, 8–9, 12–13, 16, 20, 76, 120–22, 140, 162
World War II, 32, 34, 40, 42, 44, 49, 51, 61–2, 65–6, 76, 82, 85, 93, 99, 130–31, 136–37, 139–40, 142, 145–46, 139–50, 161, 167, 173, 179, 186, 189

Yakovlev, Aleksandr, 66–7

AIRCRAFT

A-1, 186; A-2, 170; A-3, 163, 187; A3D, 187; A-4, 187; A4D, 187; A4D-5, 188; A-4E, 188; A5M, 24, 25, 42; A6M, 42–3, 61, 174; A6M2, 42; A6M5, 43; A-12, 162, 165; A-17A, 165; A-20, 170–71; A-20G, 170–71, 170–71; A-20H, 171; A-26, 170, 173; AD, 186–87; AD2, 186
Aichi D3A, 174
Airco D.H.9, 123
Airocobra, 52, 54, 56–7, 56
Airocomet, 82, 84
Amiot 352, 132
Arada Ar 234, 82
Armstrong Whitworth: Siskin, 12, 13; Siskin III, 13; Siskin IIIA(DC), 12, 13, 16; Whitley, 135, 135
Avenger, 181, 685
Avon-Sabre, 93; Mk 32, 93
Avro: Lancaster, 118–19, 146–47,

149–50; Lincoln, 150; Manchester, 146–47; Shackleton, 150; Vulcan, 160, 160
Avro Canada CF-100 Canuck, 96

B-2, 109, 124–25; B-3, 22; B5N, 179; B-7, 124, 124, 127; B-9, 124; B-10, 124–26, 125, 128; B-17, 27, 128, 128–29, 150; B-17F, 129; B-17G, 128, 130, 130–31; B-18, 128; B-24, 37, 130–31; B-25, 142, 143, 144–45; B-25A, 145; B-25D, 144–45; B-25H, 144; B-25J, 144; R-26, 142, 144–45, 144–45, 173; B-26B, 145; B-26G, 145; B-29, 146, 150, 150–51; 157; B-32, 22; B-36, 152–54, 152–53; B-36A, 152; B-45, 154; B-47, 154, 156, 160; B-47A, 156–57; B-47E, 156; B-50, 150, B-52, 154, 154–55; B-52B, 157; B-52C, 158; B-52E, 158; B-52F, 158; B-52G, 158–59; B-57, 159; B.E.2a, 9; B.E.2b, 9; Bf 109, 34–5, 44; Bf 109B, 34, 35; B109D, 35–6; Bf 109E, 36–7, 46; Bf 109F, 46, 65; Bf 109G, 37, 66–7, 137; Bf 109G2, 66; Bf 109K, 37; Bf 110, 77–8; Bf 110G4, 78, 78–9; BR.20, 135; Bre-691, 132
Baltimore, 144
Banshee, 93
Battle, 132
Bearcat, 61, 61
Beardmore, Rohrbach Inflexible, 124
Beaufighter, 76, 76, 184, 185
Beaufort I, 185
Bell: P-39 Airocobra, 52, 54, 56–7, 56; P-59 Airocomet, 82, 84; P-63 Kingcobra, 56, 57
Black Widow, 80, 81
Blenheim, 76, 132, 132–33, 185
Bloch: M.B. 131, 132; M.B. 174/175, 132; M.B. 200, 126; M.B. 200/210, 132
Boeing: B-9, 124; B-17 Flying Fortress, 128; B-17F Flying Fortress, 128–29; B-17G, 128, 130, 130–31; B-29 Superfortress, 146, 150, 150–51, 157; B-47 Stratojet, 154, 156, 160; B-47A, 156–57; B-47E, 156; B-52 Stratofortress, 154, 154–55, 156–59; B-52B, 157; B-52C, 158; B-52E, 158; B-52F, 158; B-52G, 158–59; FB-1, 15–16; F2B, 15–16; F2B-1, 16; F3B, 16; F4B, 14–16, 14; F4B1, 16; F4B4, 16; GA-1, 163, 162–63; GA-2, 163; Model 15, 15; Model 83, 15; Model 89, 15; Model 100, 15; Model 247, 21; PW-9, 15–16; XB-15, 24; XP-15, 24
Bombay, 127
Boston, 170–71, 170–71
Boulton Paul Defiant, 76
Breguet: 14A.2, 8, 9; Bre-691, 132
Brewster F2A, 52, 57, 61
Bristol: Beaufighter, 76, 76, 185; Beaufighter TF.X, 184, 185; Beaufort, 185; Beaufort I, 185; Blenheim, 76, 132, 132–33, 185; Bombay, 127; Bulldog II, 18; Bulldog M.1C, 22
British Royal Aircraft Factory; B.E.2a, 9; B.E.2b, 9
Buffalo, 52
Bulldog II, 18; Bulldog M.1C, 22

C.200, 32, 33, 40; C.202, 33, 40; C.205, 33, 40; Ca. 133, 126, 126; Ca. 313, 126, 132; CF-100, 96
Camel 2F.1, 13
Canberra, 159, 158–59
CANT Z.1007, 132, 135
Canuck, 96
Caproni, 121; Ca. 133, 126, 126;

Ca. 313, 126, 132
Commonwealth Aircraft Corporation; Avon-Sabre, 93; Mk 32, 93
Consolidated: B-24 Liberator, 37, 130–31; LB-30 Liberator, *130*; PB4Y-1, 131; PBY-2, 131; TBY Sea Wolf, 181
Convair: B-36, 152–54, *152–53*; B-36A, 152; B-36J, 153
Convair: F-102 Delta Dagger, 109; F-106 Delta Dart, *116*, 117; TF-102A Delta Dagger, *109*
Corsair, 69, *72*, 73–5, *74*
Cougar, *92*, 96
Crusader, *108*, 109
Curtiss: A-3, 163, 187; A-8 Shrike, 163; A-12 Shrike, *162*, 163, 165; A-17A Shrike, 163, 165; B-2, 109, *124–25*; F11C, 16; F11C-2, 17; F11C-3 Goshawk, 17; Falcon, 163; Hawk, 16; P-6E, 16, *16*; P.36, 32–3, *32*, 52; P-40 Warhawk, 32, 52, 56–7, *56*; P-40F, 56; SB2C Helldiver, 165, 179–85; SB2C-4, 180–81

D.1, 22; D3A, 174; D4Y, *182*; DVIII, 22; D9, 22; D-21, 22; D-27, 22; D-37, 22; D.500, 25; D.510, 25; D.520, *26*; DB-7, 170–71; DB 600, 35; DB 601A, 36; D.H.9, *123*, D.H.9A, 120–21; Do 13, 126; Do 17, 132; Do 23, 126; Do 217, 78; Do 217J, 78; Do 217N, 78
Dagger, 109, *109*
Dart, *116*, 117
Dassault Mystère IVA, *100*, *104*, 109; Mirage IIIE, *115*, 117; Mirage IVA, 161; Super Mystère 132, *104*, 109, 189
Dauntless, 179–81, *189*
Defiant, 76
De Havilland: D.H. 9A, 120–21; Mosquito, 76–8, 140, 185; Mosquito FB.VI, 185; Mk XVIII, 185; NFII, 77; NF XIX, 77; NF10, 93; NF 30, 77; PR.34, *185*; Vampire, 82, 93, *93–4*; Venom, 96
Delta: Dagger, 109, *109*; Dart, *116*, 117
Devastator, 179, 181
Dewoitine: D.1, 22; D.9, 22; D.21, 22; D.27, 22; D.37, 22; D.500, 25; D.510, 25; D.520, *26*
Dornier: Do 13, 126; Do 17, 132; Do 23, 126; Do 217, 78; Do 217j, 78
Douglas: A-1 Skyraider, 186; A3D Skywarrior, 187; A4D, 187; A-4, 187; A4D-5, 188; A-4E, 188; A-20, Havoc, 170–71; A-20G, 170–71; A-20H, 171; A-26 Invader, 170, 173, *172–73*; AD Skyhawk, 186–88; AD2, 186; B-7, 124, *124*, 127; B-18, 628; F.4D Skyray, 109; SBD Dauntless, 179–81; SND-2, *180*; TBD Devastator, 179, 181; XB-19, 127
Draken, 117, *117*

E VIII, 22
English Electric: Canberra, 159, *158–59*; Lightning, 117

F2A, 52, 57, 61; F2B, 15–16; F2B-1, *16*; F2H, 93; F3, *84*; F3B, 16; F3F, 22; F-4, *110*, 112, 116–17; F4B, 14–16, *14*, 114; F4B1, 16; F4B4, 16; F4D, 109, *114*; F4E, *113*; F4F, 52, 57, *58*, 61, 174; F4F-4, *58*; F4H, 114; F4H-1, 112, 114; F4U, 69; F4U-1, 73; F4U-1D, *72*; F4U-4, 74, *74*; F5B, *62*; F6F, 61, *61*; F8F, 61, *61*; F8U-1E, *108*; F9F, *6*, *92*, 93, 96; F11C, 16; F11C-2, 17; F11C-3, 17;

F.50, *120*; F51, 75; F-80, 93, 96; F-84, 93; F-84F, 93, *94*; F-86, 88–9, *90*, 93, 103; F-86A, 89; F-86D, *90*, 93; F-86E, 89, *90*; F-86F, 92–3; F-86L, 93; F-89, 96; F-89A, *96*; F-94, 93; F-94C, *93*; F-100, 98–9, *98*, 102–103; F-100A, 102; F-100C, 102; F-100D, *96*, 99, 102; F-100F, 102, 109; F-101, 109, *109*; F-102, 109, 109, *109*; F-104, *116*, 117; F-105, 186, 188, *189*; F-105D, *188*; F-106, *116*, 117; F-160, 121; F-220, 126, *127*; F-222, 135; FB-1, 15–16; FB-5, *94*; FB.VI, 185; FF-1, 17; FH, 93; Fw 190, 40, *42*, 67; Fw 190A-3, 40; Fw 190D/Ta 152, 40, *41*; Fw 190D/Ta 152C, *41*; Fw 190D-9, 40; Fw 190 D-12, 40
Fairey: I, *177*; II, *174*, *176*; Battle, 132; Hendon, *125*; Swordfish, 174, *176–77*
Falco, 22, *22–3*, 40
Falcon, 163
Farman: F.50, *120*; F.160, 121; F.220, 126, *127*; F.222, 135; NC 223, 135
'Farmer', 98–9, 103, *104*, 109
Fiat BR.20, 135; CR.42 Falco 22, *22–3*, 40; G.50, 33; G.55 Centauro, 33
Flying Fortress, 128, 130, *128–31*
Focke-Wulf: Fw 190 (Würger, Butcher Bird), 40, *42*, 67; Fw 190A-3, 40; Fw 190D/Ta 152, 40, *41*; Fw 190D/Ta 152C, *41*; Fw 190D-9, 40; Fw 190 D-12, 40
Fokker: D VIII, 22; E VIII, 22
Folgore, 33, 40
Fury I, 22, 51–2, *50*

GI, *121*; G3H, 144; G4M, *143*, 144; G50, 33; GA.1, 163, *162–63*; GA.2, 163; GR. Mk VIII, 140; Mk X, 140
Gladiator, *11*, 22
Gloster: Glaidator, *11*, 22; Javelin, *100*, 109; Meteor, 82, 93; Meteor F.3, *84*; Meteor NF, *12*, *82*
Goshawk, 17
Gotha Ursinus GI, *121*
Gourdon-Leseurre: B 3, 22; B 32, 22
Grumman: Avenger, 181, 185; F3F, 22; F4F Wildcat (Martlet), 52, 57, *58*, 61, 174; F6F Hellcat, 61, *61*; F8F Bearcat, 61, *61*; F9F Cougar, *6*, *92*, 96; F9F Panther, 93; FF-1, 17; TBF, 179, 181, 185

HA-1112, *38*; He 111, 132; He 162, 82; He 177, 146; He 219, 79; He 219A-5/R2, 81; Hs 123, 167; Hs 129, 167; Hs 129A, 167
Halifax, 146; II, *147*
Hampden, 132
Handley Page: 0/100, *121*; 0/400, 120–21; Halifax, 146, *147*; Hampden, 132; Harrow, 126; V/1500, 120; Victor, 159–60, *161*
Harrow, 126
Hart, 143
Havoc, 170, *170–71*
Hawker: 22, 44, *48*, 49, *50*, 51–2, 96, 120, 143; Fury 1, 22, 51–2, *50*; Hunter, 96, *186–87*, 189; Hurricane, 32, 44, *48*, 49, *50*, 51, 66–7, 120; Hurricane IIC, *48*; Hurricane IID, 44; Sea Fury, 52, *52*, 96; Tempest, 51, 96, 170; Tempest II, 51; Tempest V/VI, 51; Typhoon, 49, 51, 170
Hayabusa, 42
Heinkel: He 111, 132; He 162, 82; He 177, 146; He 219, 79
Hellcat, 61, *61*
Helldiver, 165, 179–80, 185
Hendon, *125*

Hesnchel: Hs-123, 167; 129, 167; 129A, 167
Hien (Swallow), 43
Hispano HA-1112, *38*
Hunter, 96, *186–87*, 189
Hurricane, 32, 44, *48*, 49, *50*, 66–7, 120

I-14, 25; I-16, 4, 25, 28–9, 32, 65; I-153, *18*, 22
Ilyushin: Il-2, 168–69; Il-2M, 168; Il-2m3, 169, *168–69*; Il-8, 169; Il-10, 160; Il-28, 154
Invader, 170, 173, *172;73*

JI, 162; J2M, 43, *43*; J29, 93, 96; J35, 117, *117*
'Judy', 182
Junkers: DI, 22; JI, 162; Ju 52/3m, 126; Ju 87, 165, *166*, 167; Ju 87B, 167; Ju 87B-1, *164–65*; Ju 87D, 167; Ju 87G, 167; Ju 88, 76, 78, *78–9*, 132, 136–42, *136–37*, 167; 88A, 78; 88-A4, 137–38, *137*, 142; 88-A5, *138*, 88A-17, 138; 88C, 138; 88-C6, 78; 88D, 139; 88G, 79; 88G-7, 79; 88G-76, 79; 88H, 139; 88P, 138; 88R, 79; 88S, 139; 88S-1, 139; 88T, 139; Ju 188, 140; Ju 288, 140; Ju 388, 140

Kawanishi N1K, 43
Kawasaki: Ki-21, 144; Ki-27, 25, 42; Ki-43, 42–3; Ki-44, 43; Ki-48, 144; Ki-49, 144; Ki-61 Hien (Swallow), 43; Ki-84, 43
Kingcobra, *56*, 57

LaGG-1, 66; LaGG-3, 66; La-5, 66; La-5N, 66; La-9, 66; La-11, 66; LB-30, *130*; LeO 451, 132, *134–35*; LeO 206, 135; LVG C VI, *8*
Lancaster, *118–19*, 146–47, 149, 149–50
Lavochkin, 66
Liberator, 37, 130–31, *130*
Lightning (English Electric), 117
Lightning (Lockheed), 56, 61–2, *62*, 81
Lincoln, 150
Lioré-et-Olivier: LeO 206, 135; LeO 451, 132, *134–35*
Lockheed: F-5B Lightning, 56, 61–2, *62*, 81; F-80 Shooting Star, 93, 96; F-94 Starfire, 93; F-94C Starfire, *94*; F-104 Starfighter, *116*, 117; P-38 Lightning, 56, 61, 81; P38J, *62*; P-38L, 62; P-38M, *80*; P-80 Shooting Star, 82, *82*, 86

M-4, 160–61, *160–61*; M.B. 131, 132; M.B. 174/175, 132; M.B. 200, 126; M.B. 200/210, 132; Me-163, 85; Me-262, 82, *82*, 85; Me-262B-1a/VI, *82*; M.S. 406, 32
Macchi: C.200 Saetta, *32*, 33, 40; C.202 Folgore, 33, 40; C.205 Veltro, 33, 40
McDonnell: F2H Banshee, 93; F4 Phantom II, *110*, 112, 114–17; F4B, 114; F4D, *114*; F4E Phantom, *113*; F4H, 114; F-101 Voodoo, 109, *109*; FH Phantom, 93
Manchester, 146–47
Marauder, 142, 144–45, *144–45*
Martin: B-10, 124–26, *125*, 128; B.26 Marauder, 142, 144–45, *144–45*; B-57, 159; Baltimore, 144; Maryland, 144; XB-907A, 22
Messerschmitt: Bf 109, 34–5, 44; Bf 109B, *34*, 35; Bf 109D, 35–6; Bf 109E, 36–7, 46; Bf 109F, 46, 65; Bf 109G, 37, *137*; Bf 109 G-2, 66–7;

Bf 109K, 37; Bf 110, 77–8; Bf 110G-4, 78, *78–9*; DB 600, 35; DB 601A, 36; Me 262, 82, *82*, 85
Meteor, 82, *82*, *84*, 93
MiG: -1, 65-6; -3, 65; -15, 88–9, *88*, 93, 103; -15bis, 92, 103; -17, 96; -19, 98–9, 103, 109; -19PM, *104*; -21, 112, *112–13*, 116–17
Mirage IIIE, *115*, 117; IVA, 161
Mitchell, 142, *143*, 144–45
Mitsubishi: A5M, *24*, 25, 42; A5M Reisen (Zero), 42–3, 61, 174; A6M2 Model 21, 42; A6M5, *43*; G3M, 144; G4M, *143*, 144; J2M, 43, *43*
Mosquito, 30, 76–8, 93, 140, 185
Mustang, *68*, 69, *70*, 72, 75, 130, *157*
Mystère, *100*, *104*, 109

NA-73,ʹ69; NC 223, 135; NF, *12*, *82*; NF II, 77; NF XIX, 77; NF 10, *93*; NF 12, *82*; NF 30, 77; N1K, 43
Nakajima: B5N, 179; Ki-21, 144; Ki-27, 25, 42; Ki-43 Hayabusa (Peregrine Falcon), 42–3; Ki-44, 43; Ki-49, 144; Ki-84, 43
Nieuport 29, 12
North American: B-25 Mitchell, 142, *143*, 144–45; B-25D, 144–45; B-25H, 144; B-25J, 144; B-45 Tornado, 154; F-86 Sabre, 88–9, *90*, 93, 103; F-86A, 89; F86D Sabre Dog, *90*, 93; F-86E, 89, *90*; F-86F, 92–3; F-86L, 93; F-100 Super Sabre, 98–9, *98*, 102–103; F-100A, 102; F-100C, 102; F-100D Super Sabre, *96*, 99, 102; F-100F, 102, 109; NA-73, 69; P-51 Mustang, 69, 75, 130; P-51A, *68*; P-51B, 69; P-51B, 69, 72; P-51D, *70*, 72; P-51H, 72; P-82 Twin Mustang, 72; RB-45C, *157*; TP-51D, *70*
Northrop: 2, 163; 8A, 163; F-89 Scorpion, 96; F-89A, *96*; P-61 Black Widow, *80*, 81

P-6E, 16–17, *16*; P-12, 14–16; P-12C, 16; P-12E, 16; P-12F, 16; P-26, 24; P-26C, *22–3*; P.36, 32–3, *32*, 52; P-38, 56, 61, 81; P-38J, *62*; P-38L, 62; P-38M, *80*; P-39, 52, *54*, 56–7, *56*; P-40, 32, 52, 56–7, *56*; P-40F, 56; P-47, 32, 62, 64; P-51, 69, 75; P51A, *68*; P-51B, 69, 72, 130; P51D, *70*, 72; P-51H, 72; P-59, 82, *84*; P-61, *80*, 81; P-63, *56*, 57; P-70, 171; P-80, 82, *86*; P-82, 72; P-80, 82, *82*, *86*; P-80C, *82*; P.108, 146, *148*; PBY-2, 131; PB4Y-1, 131; Pe-2, 168–69, *169*; Pe-3, 169; Pe-8, 146, *148–49*; PR.34, *185*; PW-9, 15–16; PZL P-7, 24
Panther, 83
Petlyakov: Pe-2, 168–69, *169*; Pe-3, 169; Pe-8, 146, *148–49*
Phantom, 93, *110*, *113*, 112, 114–17, *114*
Piaggio P.108, 146, *148*
Polikarpov I-14, 25; I-16, 25, 28, 32; I-16 Type 4, 28; I-153, *18*, 22; Type 24, 28–9
Potez 633, 132

RB-45C, *157*
Reggiane: Re. 2000, 33; Re. 2005, Sagittario, 33
Republic: F-84 Thunderjet, 93; F-84F Thunderstreak, 93, *94*; F-105 Thunderchief, 186, 188, *189*
Rohrbach Inflexible, 124

SB-2, 144; SB2C, 179–80, 185; SB2C-4m 180–81; SB2C-4E, 81; SB2U, 179; SB2U-1, *178*; SBC, 180; SBD, 179–81; SBD-2, *180*; SBD-5, 180; SBG, 180; S.M.79, *133*, 135;

S.M.81, 126; S.M.84, *133*; SO 4050, *187*, 189; Su-7, 189; Su-9/11, 116
Saab 29A Tunnan, *96*; J29, 93, 96; J35 Draken, 117, *117*
Sabre, 88–9, *90*, 103
Sabre Dog, *90*, 93
Saetta, *32*, 33, 40
Salamander, 162
Savoia-Marchetti: S.M.79, 135; S.M.81 Pipistrello, 126; S.M.84, *133*
Scorpion, 96, *96*
Seafire, 46
Seafang, 49
Sea Fury, 52, *52*, 96
Sea Wolf, 181
Seversky P-35, 32–3, *33*, 52
Shackleton, 150
Shooting Star, 82, *82*, *86*, 93, 96
Short, Stirling, 146, *146*
Shrike, *162*, 163
Shturmovik, 168–69, *168–69*
Sikorsky Ilya Maurometz, *120*
Siskin: *12*, 13; III, 13; IIIA(DC), 13, *12–13*, 16
Skyhawk, 186–88
Skyraider, 186
Skyray, 109
Skywarrior, 187
SNCASO SO 4050 Vautour, 189
Sopwith Camel 2F.1, 13; T.F.2 Salamander, 162
Spiteful, 49, 64

Spitfire, 1, 20, *30*, 37, 44–6, 48–9, 120
Starfighter, *116*, 117
Stirling Mk III, 146, *146*
Starfire, 93, *94*
Stratofortess, 154, 156–59
Stratojet, 154, 156
Stuka, 165, *164–66*, 167
Sud Aviation SO. 4050 Vautour, *187*, 189
Sukhoi: Su-7, 189; Su-9/11, 116
Superfortress, 146, 150, 157
Supermarine: Seafang, 49; Seafire, 46; Spiteful, 49, 64; Spitfire, 1, 20, *30*, 37, 44–6, 48–9, 120; Mk IA, 45–6; Mk II, 46; Mk VI, 46; Mk VII, 46; Mk VIII, 46, 48–9; Mk IX, 46, 48; Mk XII, 49; Mk XIV, 49; Mk 21, 49; Mk 22, 49; Mk 24, 49
Super Mystère, *104*, 109, 189
Super Sabre, 96, 98–9, *98*, 103–104
Susei (Comet), *182*
Swallow, 43
Swordfish, 174, *176–77*

T.17, *158–59*
TB-1, 125; TBD, 179, 181; TBF, 179, 181, 185; TBU, 181; TBY, 181; TF.2, 162; TF-102A, *109*; TF.X, *184*, 185; TP-51D, *70*; Tu-2, 144; Tu-4, 157, 160; Tu-14, 154; Tu-20, 160–61; Tu-28, 116
Tempest, 51, 96, 170
Thunderbolt, 32, 62, 64; Thunderbolt

I, *69*; Thunderbolt XP-47J, 64; Thunderchief, 186, 188, *189*; Thunderjet, 93; Thunderstreak, 93, *94*
Tornado, 154, *157*
Tunnan, *96*
Tupolev: I-14, 25; I-16, 25, 28–9, 32; SB-2, 144; TB-1, 125; Tu-2, 144; Tu-4, 157, 160; Tu-14, 154; Tu-20, 160–61; Tu-28, 116
Twin Mustang, 72
Typhoon, 49, 51

Ursinus G I, *121*

V/1500, 120
Valentia, *122–23*
Valiant, 159, *161*
Vampire, 82, 93, *93–4*
Vautour, *187*, 189
Veltro, 33, 40
Venom, 96
Vickers: Valiant, 159, *161*; Valentia, *122–23*; Virginia, 122; Warwick, 141; Wellesley, 132; Wellington, 132, 136, 140–42; Mk 10, 140, 142–43
Victor, 159–60
Vindicator, *178*, 179, *181*
Voodoo, 109, *109*
Vought: F4U Corsair, 69, 73–5; F4U-1, 73; F4U-1D, *72*; F4U1-E Crusader, *108*, 109, F4U-4, 74, *74*;

SB2U Vindicator, *178*, 179; SB2U-1 Vindicator, *181*; TBU, 181
Vulcan, 160, *160*

Wapiti, 131
Warhawk (Tomahawk/Kittyhawk), 32, 52, 56, *56*
Warwick, 141
Wellesley, 132
Wellington, 132, 136, 140–42, *138–41*
Westland, Wapiti, 131
Whitley, 135, *135*
Wildcat (Martlet), 52, 57, *58*, 61, 174

XB-15, 127; XB-19, 127; XB-907A, 22; XP-15, *24*; XP-47J, 64

Yakovlev: Yak-1, 66–8; Yak-1M, 67, *68*; Yak-3, 67–8, *66*; Yak-3U, 67; Yak-7, 68; Yak 7A, 68; Yak 7B, 68, *68*; Yak-9, 68; Yak-9B, 68; Yak-9D, 68; Yak-9DD, 68; Yak-9FK, 68; Yak-9L, 68; Yak-9P, 68; Yak-9PVO, 68; Yak-9R, 68; Yak 9T, 37, 68; Yak 9T-45, 68; Yak 9U, 68; Yak 9UF, 68; Yak-25, 109; Yak-28, 116
Yokosuka O4Y, *182*

Z. 1007, 132, 135
Zero, 42–3, *43*, 61, 174

ACKNOWLEDGMENTS

The publishers and researchers would like to thank the following individuals and organisations who supplied illustrations for this book. For reasons of space alone, some references have been abbreviated as follows:
Boeing Airplane Co—Boeing
Blitz/Librair Photo-Archive, N Wales—BL
British Aerospace, UK—BAe
Fanatique de l'Air, Paris—FA
Stuart Howe, London—SH
Imperial War Museum, London—IWM
Military Archive & Research Services, London—MARS
Musee de l'Air, Paris—MA
US Air Force Photo—USAF

Front cover: J Batchelor. Back cover: IWM. p1: BAe. 2–3: SH. 4–5: IWM. 6–7: SVAS. 8: IWM. 9:MA. 10–11: SVAS. 12–13: BL. 14–15: Boeing/MARS. 16: Boeing/MARS. 17: USAF/MARS. 18–19: MA/FA. 19: BL. 20–21: BAe/MARS. 22: IWM. 23: Boeing/MARS. 24–25 (top): IWM. 24–25 (btm): Boeing/MARS. 26: BL. 26–27: MA/FA. 27: SH. 28–29: IWM. 30–31: IWM. 32 (top): Italian Air Force/MARS. 32 (btm): USAF/MARS. 33: USAF/MARS. 34–37: BL. 38–39: SH. 40: Fujifotos. 41 (top): BL. 41 (btm): IWM. 42: SH. 43: USAF/MARS. 44–45: Vickers Ltd/MARS. 46–47: IWM. 48–49: BAe. 50: BAe/MARS. 50–51: IWM. 52–53: BAe. 54–55: Bell Aerospace-Textron/MARS. 56–57 (top): BL. 56–57 (btm): Bell Aerospace-Textron/MARS. 58–59: Michael O'Leary. 59: Grumman Aerospace/MARS. 60–61: Grumman Aerospace/MARS. 61: Martin Marietta Corp/MARS. 62–62: Lockheed California/MARS. 64–65: IWM. 66–67: MA/FA. 68: IWM. 68–69: Rockwell International/MARS. 71: Michael O'Leary. 72–73: Vought Corp/MARS. 74–75: SH. 75: Vought Corporation/MARS. 76–77: BL. 78–79: BL. 79: IWM. 80: BL. 80–81: Northrop Corporation/MARS. 82–83: USAF/MARS. 82–83: IWM. 83: Lockheed California/MARS. 83: BAe. 84: Bell Aerospace-Textron/MARS. 84–85: BL. 86–87: Lockheed California/MARS. 88–89: Finnish Air Force/MARS. 90: BL. 90–91: Michael O'Leary. 91: BL. 92–93: Grumman Aerospace/MARS. 93: BAe/MARS. 94: Fairchild Republic/MARS. 94–95: Lockheed California/MARS. 95: British Aerospace. 96: Saab-Scania/MARS. 96–97: Northrop Corporation/MARS. 96–97: Canadian Armed Forces/MARS. 97: Rockwell International/MARS. 98–99: Rockwell International/MARS. 100: Avions M Dassault/MARS. 102–103: Crown Copyright (RAF)/MARS. 104–105: Avions M Dassault/MARS. 104: Novosti Press Agency. 105: Avions M Dassault/MARS. 106–107: Vought Corporation/MARS. 108/109: McDonnell Douglas Corp/MARS. 109: General Dynamics/MARS. 110–111: McDonnell Douglas Corp/MARS. 112–113: US Navy/MARS. 113: USAF/MARS. 114–115: Avions M Dassault/MARS. 115: USAF/MARS. 116: BL. 116–117: General Dynamics/MARS. 117: Saab-Scania/MARS. 118–119: IWM. 120 (top): IWM. 120 (btm): MARS. 121 (top): IWM. 121 (btm): Bundesarchiv. 122–123: Vickers Limited/MARS. 123: SH. 124: USAF/MARS. 124–125 (top): Martin Marietta/MARS. 124–125 (btm): USAF/MARS. 125: Westland Aircraft Co. 126: Italian Air Force/MARS. 126–127: BAe/MARS. 127: ECP Armees, Paris. 128–129: Boeing/MARS. 129: USAF/MARS. 130–131: USAF/MARS. 131: SH. 132–133: BAe/MARS. 133: Italian Air Force/MARS. 134: BAe/MARS. 134–135: BL. 136–137: IWM. 137: BL. 138–139: MARS. 140–141 (top): Vickers Limited/MARS. 140–141: IWM. 142–143: SH. 143: BL. 144–145: USAF/MARS. 146: Short Bros. 146–147: IWM. 148: Italian Air Force/Mars. 148–149: IWM. 150–151: SH.152: BL. 152–153: General Dynamics/MARS. 154–155 (top): USAF/MARS. 154–155 (btm): SH. 156–157: Boeing/MARS. 157: Rockwell International/MARS. 158–159: Crown Copyright /RAF)/MARS. 160–161: Crown Copyright (RAF). 161 (btm): Vickers Limited/MARS. 163: USAF/MARS. 162–163: Boeing/MARS. 164–165: IWM. 166: MARS. 168–169: IWM. 170–171: SH. 171: IWM. 172–173: USAF/MARS. 174–175: SH. 176: IWM. 177 (top): David Tytler. 177 (btm): IWM. 178: Vought Corp/MARS. 178–179: SH. 180: US Navy/MARS. 181 (top): Vought Corp/MARS. 181 (btm): BL. 182: Michael O'Leary. 182–183: SH. 184–185: BL. 186–187: Crown Copyright (RAF)/MARS. 187: G Bousquet/FA. 188–189: Fairchild Republic/MARS.